CHANDAN DESHMUKH

SIX SECRETS SMART STUDENTS DON'T TELL YOU

westland ltd

61, II Floor, Silverline Building, Alapakkam Main Road, Maduravoyal, Chennai 600095

93, I Floor, Sham Lal Road, Daryaganj, New Delhi 110002

First published in India by westland ltd 2014

15 14 13 12 11 10 9 8 7

ISBN: 978-93-84030-16-2

Typeset: PrePSol Enterprise Pvt. Ltd.

Printed at Radha Press, New Delhi

Contents

Dedication v

Acknowledgements vi

Prologue.. viii

Chapter One: The Mother of All Secrets 1

Chapter Two: Zone-Breaking–Ceremony 6

Chapter Three: Secret #1: Load-Aim-Shoot........................... 9

Chapter Four: Secret #2: Peacock with Two Chairs.............. 22

Chapter Five: Secret #3: A 500 Page Book –
On The Tip of Your Tongue 37

Chapter Six: Secret #4: Tuition Fees in the Bank 51

Chapter Seven: Secret #5: Stand and Deliver....................... 69

Chapter Eight: Secret #6: Time Machine............................. 87

Chapter Nine: 10 Step-By-Step Approaches
To Be The Star Of The Class This Year................................. 96

Chapter Ten: Brownie Points.. 109

What happened next?... 116

Dedication

This book is for you. Yes, you, the one reading this.

P.S: I know how it feels when you pick up a book, flip to the dedication, and find that, once again, the author has dedicated a book to someone else and not to you.

Not this time.

Acknowledgements

If this book is said to be a tree, I am indebted to the below souls who nurtured its growth.

Charan Deshmukh, my loving brother. To get his prompt in-the-face review about what I had written, I would wake him up abruptly even at midnight; sometimes bang the door while he was bathing, and bore him during dinner!

My Parents, Ramesh and Srimathi. Thanks for all the love, blessings and tolerating the sound of typing. Also my Fiancée Meghana, for keeping me grounded and unbiased reviewing.

All my School and College teachers and in particular, MC Nagaraj Sir of Kumarans PU college, Bangalore. For teaching me more about life than Sanskrit lessons, for the preliminary edit and invaluable inputs in creating this book.

Anuj Bahri, my agent, for his sheer confidence in 'Six Secrets'.

Westland Ltd, led by Gautam Padmanabhan, for publishing me and sharing the dream.

Karthik Venkatesh, my editor. He could be a primary teacher with his patience. If you are a debut author and lucky enough to get him on your side, your job is a cake walk.

Gunjan Ahlawat for a catchy cover design. Krishna Nair for ensuring that this book reaches you in every possible way.

Friends who taught me about smart studying, knowledgeable authors and speakers such as Shakuntala Devi, Dale Carnegie, Kevin Paul, Nina Sunday, Bharath Chandra etc. Their ideas led me to brainstorm and deep dive.

L&T Infotech team, Relatives and friends who are with me during all my crests and troughs.

You, the reader, for the leap of faith in picking up the book of a debut author.

Chandan Deshmukh
www.ChandanDeshmukh.com

Prologue

There are three types of students in the world:

- *The Excuse-me*
- *The Halo*
- *The Cocktail*

The differentiation doesn't depend on their grade or age or where they sit in class. It is all in the attitude.

'The Excuse-me's' are the guys who think-up excuses even in the best conditions needed to perform and are generally apathetic towards life and studies. They seem to be related to a species of sheep – if one amongst the flock says, "I can't," you will immediately hear a million echoes buzzing around.

What would they do if you questioned them about their low scores? No prizes for guessing – you will hear a few more excuses:

 "My relatives had come from America and disturbed my studies" → "My parents are uneducated, so I have no one to guide me" → "The teacher didn't evaluate my answer sheet properly" → "Unfortunately, I joined *Ramesh Tutorials*. If I had been admitted to *Suresh Tutorials*, I would have been a topper by now" → "My *kundali* has a *dosh*".

And so on! 'Passive' is a kind term for them.

However, students who have **'The Halo'** play a different ball game altogether. They are the exact opposites of The Excuse-me students. They amalgamate thinking and doing. Learning unique skills and imagining their prospective growth-graph rising, is their favorite pastime. The hunger for success bubbles is in their blood and if provided support, they brook no boundaries. They play the game of life passionately and always ask – *what's next?* Problems do haunt this set of students as well; however, the attitude to face issues is the decisive factor and such students prove themselves ready to meet any challenges. The Halo students are the need of the hour.

The Cocktail? – Quite self-explanatory. This category of students are aligned to the thin line that separates The Halo and The Excuse-me. Their number is growing exponentially and yes, they are vital for society to remain stable.

The idea of this book is not to pigeon-hole anybody into these three categories. The motto of this book is to ease students' efforts in coping with their curriculum and get them better grades. Each student in the class, no matter if they were a topper or a low-scorer in the last exam, stands on the same starting line at the beginning of a new academic year. It is the effort you put in, which determines your position as you approach the finishing line!

As a whole, the big picture is simple. Though it makes students happy to point fingers, the adage remains true:

'There may be bad teachers, but not bad students.'

Chapter One:

The Mother of All Secrets

"I have never let my schooling interfere with my education."

– Mark Twain

The Indian Education system is similar to the Indian Railways.

	Indian Railways	**Indian Education System**
1	People sleep on berths	Students sleep on desks
2	Railway tracks are fixed	Studying tracks are fixed
3	Bogies are laid back to back	Classes are conducted back to back
4	Trains have reservations	Classes have reservations
5	People de-board the train at their stop	Students de-board studies when marks stop

"If you attempt to deviate from the line, you will go nowhere, don't be left behind!" Parents warn.

"Turning points are critical, prepare well!" Teachers caution.

"The fees have increased, you have no choice!" Blabber the educational institutions.

Zoom in, and you will see the pitiful students juggling to impress all the above categories!

Though India's literacy rate jumped from 5% in 1901 to 74% in 2011, we have been instructed 'TO' study, but never taught 'HOW' to study. Catch hold of any passing student and interrogate him for his secret to studying, and he is bound to look around stealthily and utter, "Be it any subject, I by-heart the notes". I belonged to the same tribe as well, till THAT day – which made me re-think all my assumptions on the curriculum.

Which was that horrible, *horrendous* day which brings shivers down the spine of any average student?

A Parent-Teacher meeting!

I, then a 14 year old, was accompanied by my mom to collect the marks card of the mid-term exams, on a Saturday afternoon. I had on a timidly optimistic smile, as the arrival of my father to such a felicitous gathering had been avoided. If he had come along, it would have become more of a 'slaughtering', than a meeting.

I was a below-average student, sitting in the fourth row, supporting the wall. Laughing at the pranks of the last benchers, and getting help from the front benchers during a test was a daily affair.

As soon as my class teacher Mrs. Sunitha noticed me entering the staff room, she stood up from her chair and bounded towards me like a dog catcher chasing a street dog. She was a highly seasoned Math teacher who felt students could be mended ONLY by punishment. She could have tamed a lion with her piercing gaze. Her punishments would always have the following prefixes:

- *Whyy are you laaaffing? Tell me also no, I also waant to laaf.*
- *Whyy do you camm to school if you don't lyke stadiees?*
- *Ees thees a class or a fiiish maarket?*
- *I yam taaking to you vonly. Whyy are you looking baack an all?*
- *Yuvar juniarrs are mach mach saylent than you. Larrn from them noo.*
- *Whyy you don't bring vomework? Do you farget lunch baax?*
- *Ai will thrrow you aut of the claas.*

Her heavy-set features and long hair went well with her attitude. She instantly showered her updated complaints onto mom, like a wife complaining about her mother-in-law to her husband.

The other staff members nodded their heads, acknowledging every complaint. The nodding frequency would double every time Mrs. Sunitha paused to take a deep breath. Her usual high-pitched tone not only tore my sensitive eardrum apart, but also took away my mom's smile.

The complaints covered a wide spectrum: right from getting 5 out of 25 in Social Science, being a chatterbox, making animal sounds and then pretending innocence, non-submission of innumerable homework assignments, standing last in my unit test results, etc. The Sonometer's reading would be at its maximum if measured at that moment. "He was also caught pulling Tina's hair band during my class," she uttered. Involuntarily, I frowned. I never wanted this last complaint to be spilled out, especially to mom.

Now came the icing on the cake. The heartless Math teacher unveiled my midterm exam score card. It read 'C+'. As if adding a '+' in the card would have made my future resume strong. The whole staff was awaiting mom's expression as if at a post-match presentation ceremony where either I or the teacher would be felicitated.

Unusually the staffroom turned silent. I could hear the breeze. Seconds passed like hours. I never knew that silence could be THIS silent!

I raised my head in confusion.

Mom was crying. Tears flowed from both her eyes. She stood still and didn't even wipe them off.

This was the last thing I had expected. My love for mom couldn't tolerate her silent cry. The whole world turned blue. I didn't want anything in the world except to bring her comfort. As my fists firmed, I felt like shouting out loud, "Ma, don't cry, please hit me, punish me till you are satisfied, I can bear that, but not this silent cry!"

She swallowed a lump of anguish. She was disappointed.

I wished I could run away from the world. Far away. Where my mom's sorrow would be invisible and none could perceive my agony.

I had a new enemy – Mrs. Sunitha.

Charged to 11000 volts, my only aim was to bring back the lost sheen on mom's face and prove Mrs. Sunitha wrong. That prompted me to explore the terrain of smart studying. I met diverse people, as I preferred studying brilliant students rather than textbooks. And I shadowed all the activities undertaken by top-ranked nerds – right from the way they listened in class, the way they tied their shoelaces, the way they chewed the back of their pencils, to the way they brainstormed. Bribing them with delicious home food from my lunch box was the usual method applied.

I realised their best kept secrets.

They are explicitly unveiled in this book, just for you.

The names mentioned have been changed on request and I have no intention to hurt anybody. A few situations described here relate to my real life, but the timelines may differ. A few are made-up to add spice to the story. The flow may seem filmy, but that's thanks to the fairy tales my parents narrated while feeding me in childhood.

Read. Follow. Succeed.

***

Chapter Two:

Zone-Breaking–Ceremony

"The difference between ordinary and extra-ordinary is that little extra."

–Anonymous

In India, most auspicious ceremonies have the custom of coconut breaking coupled with it. The ego and the other negative aspects of life are interpreted as the shell and progress as the kernel of the coconut. In short, by breaking the shell, our spirit is opened-up to prosperity.

Don't you think that acquiring the skills to score better is auspicious as well?

All our potential is predominantly embalmed in the shell named 'comfort zone'. Once you go through the 'Zone-breaking–Ceremony', you crack yourself out of these limitations.

Moving on without practically following the subsequent steps would be like a soldier diving into the battlefield without ammunition i.e. a blunder. Read the steps slowly as you practise in real-time; visualise them by closing your eyes.

Step 1: Spread a single sheet of newspaper on the floor.

Step 2: Stand on the sheet.

Step 3: Imagine that this area of the newspaper is your comfort zone, and you are virtually trapped within it. Feel the warmth in your toes. As long as you are here, you have no worries, no studies, no thinking and no progress either. There will be no accomplishments as well.

But that is not our intent!

Step 4: Step out of the comfort zone!

Step 5: Perceive that you are out, enchanted in the fresh air. Take a few deep breaths. Realise that the world is at your disposal. Challenges are now your daily diet!

You can conquer any milestone if you apply your mind. You can study a difficult chapter in a jiffy; your concentration is at the peak and scoring marks is as easy as tearing a page in half.

Step 6: Scrunch-up the comfort zone (the newspaper sheet) and throw it in the dustbin.

Step 7: Go, conquer the world.

Redo the above steps whenever you feel down and want a recharge.

Note:

- Take an old newspaper sheet; else you will be discomfited to see your father chasing you around the house.
- Either do this exercise alone or explain this to mom prior to attempting it, else she could call a doctor to treat you, and a lawyer to sue me.
- Standing on paper seems warm, but is not recommended for a long time.
- The comfort zone will not hold you back in throwing the sheet into the dustbin, I promise.
- And yes, this exercise definitely helps. Zero ambiguity.

***

Chapter Three:

Secret #1: Load-Aim-Shoot

"Vision without action is a daydream. Action without vision is a nightmare."

– Japanese proverb

Feb 7th, 1999 India vs. Pakistan test match, 2nd Innings, Ferozeshah Kotla Cricket Stadium, Delhi.

Inzamam-Ul-Haq on strike with the bat, Anil Kumble with the ball. Pak is 309 runs away from an emphatic series win. India needs 8 more wickets.

Kumble spins the ball in his hands, laser eyes target the opponent's scalp. The crowd cheers, "Indiaaaa… India!" The sweat from Inzamam's forehead flows down the inner brim of the helmet to his cheek and finally evaporates on the dry pitch.

Kumble takes a brisk run up and delivers the ball. Humongous Inzamam, taking the short ball for granted, hits it with a wristy shot to the boundary. The sweet sound of the ball hitting the middle of the willow reverberates throughout the stadium amidst silence from the Indian crowd. The umpire signals a boundary. Kumble slaps his forehead and says, "I knew this would go for a boundary!"

Kumble again with the ball. This time, he closes his eyes and visualises that he is bowling the opponent out with his succeeding delivery. He practises the same mindset which had got him his last wicket. He also visualises that he punches his fist in the air in celebration.

Motivated, Kumble opens his eyes, narrows his eyes at the off-stump, and nods his head as if he was signalling the stumps to watch it. He takes a longer run up, assisted by his flexible thumb he rolls the ball in the air slowing down the pace. Ball on to the pitch, leg spin, and thud! There falls the off stump! Inzamam walks to the pavilion in despair.

Acknowledging his previous visualisation, Kumble thumps his fist in the air and screams, "I knew this would be my wicket!" Up goes the umpire's forefinger and the whole crowd erupts in celebration. A rush of energy soars across each nook and corner of the stadium. Later in the day, India wins the test match and Kumble is crowned the Man of the Match.

What was the difference between those two balls delivered by Kumble?

It is the mindset.

All things happen twice – once in the mind and once in reality.

Vimal paused for a moment to observe my reaction to his theatrical narration. I was lost in his tale, and my mouth was still open, imbibing the moral. He was a regular 3rd ranking student of the class and one of my close friends.

"So what's your secret to scoring well?" I came to the point.

"Uhmmmm..." His eyes were explicitly searching for my lunch box.

I sadly unpacked it from my bag. I had promised to share my lunch, a favourite among my classmates – *Chole Batura*. A lip-smacking dish my mom prepares which can make even the best chefs go nuts.

We South Indian folk love tangy North Indian cuisine and the reason is still unknown.

"Here you go," I put the box on the desk. A sudden beam of light seemed to illuminate his pockmarked face.

"What's the secret?" I asked him again. This time in a more confident, emphatic tone, as I had bribed him. Now it was his turn to share.

"The secret is…" he scanned all 360 degrees of the surroundings to find out if anyone else was in the class. Why would anyone else choose to be in class during lunch break?

"Continue please, no more pauses," I insisted.

"My secret is goal setting," he uttered.

Ah! He was lying. The sky fell on my head. The ocean waves stopped. The flying birds stopped midair. The breeze paused in its flow. I had lost my favourite lunch. I didn't anticipate this.

"Mere goal setting is your secret? Come on! Goal setting has been there for ages; it is a known tool and doesn't work!" I shook my right hand in a typical rejection-in-Indian-style gesture.

"What else should it be? So you expect that the secret to score more should be witchcraft? A secret pen? Or an invisible magic uncle who helps during exams?" he sniggered.

"Ok. Goal setting! I should be declared insane for listening to this. Can you please elaborate? I am not convinced," I said.

"We will reach nowhere by blindly running on without any plan or strategy. Get up, go to school/college, then to tutorials, come home and sleep. Scribble nonsense in the exam, expect a bumper grade, get scoldings, and be miserable. This is *aam zindagi* – a fire fight. If you want to reach the top, start doing things differently!"

He paused to tear-up a big piece of *batura*, dipped it into a generous amount of *chole* and started to chew. Though a small piece of coriander was stuck to his front tooth, it didn't bother me as surprisingly, he was talking sense.

He continued, "Before buying an apartment, we examine a model flat. Prior to laying the foundation for a huge building, a miniature structure is created. Any business uses a business plan. Furthermore, a family of four which wants to go to Delhi for a 5-day vacation in April, starts planning at least from November of the previous year! If 5 days require 6 months of planning, isn't a solid blueprint necessary for a lifespan?"

I fell for the last sentence he spoke. But I had questions. He paused his words for another bite. Though my empty stomach was grumbling loudly, my brain was filling-up with splendid food.

"*Long ago, there was a competition...*" he changed his tactics; he was dexterous at influencing me.

"The person who could climb the 48-storeyed Rose Towers first, would win the race. Folks in hundreds had gathered to witness the rare spectacle. 12 youths had volunteered to compete the climb. The starting line was 300 metres away from the building.

As soon as the referee raised his pistol and shot high in the air, the dozen started running as though their life depended on it. The crowd's cheer was audible even to the neighbouring localities.

Climbing 48 sets of staircases is no child's play. Stamina, skill, confidence and self-motivation are mandatory even to imagine climbing such a building. It consumes not less than 30 minutes for a well-built person to ascend it, as one tends to slow down with the number of floors.

However, a participant managed to make it within 5 minutes, raised his hand and screamed his heart out in celebration!

There was pin drop silence in the crowd. Nobody seemed delighted. No applause, no hurrahs. Instead, the mass seemed to boo him.

He had climbed the wrong building.

Are we not doing the same thing? Isn't it high time for us to change? We need to focus on the right building first! What say?" he challenged.

The answer was yes. A dark fog now seemed cleared. I wanted to set goals instantly.

"Ok, my goal is to become a good student!" I said confidently, wanting to impress him. I suppose he should be convinced with this.

"Hold your horses, Mr. Good Student. There is a protocol to set goals," he paused.

"Chennai Police ate Ice-cream!" he exclaimed.

I was flabbergasted. The *Channa Batura* was almost done with.

Is this guy insane? When did I ask about the Chennai police? When did they eat? IPL Cricket season was far away. Why are all nerdy guys strange? I made bemused faces in puzzlement.

"Chennai Police ATE Ice-cream. This is the rule for goal setting!" His pitch got lower. The secret was being revealed.

***

"Chennai Police ATE Ice-cream" is an Acronym for the rules of goal setting. C-P-A-T-E-I.

C: Constructive, P: Practical, A: Arithmetical, T: Time-bound, E: Elastic, I: Individual.

These are the six ingredients for a perfect goal.

Skipping steps without analysing each parameter would be like window shopping – you go home empty-handed.

C – Constructive:

Sumit is a 2nd ranking student in the 9th standard. For a long time, his efforts at obtaining the 1st rank have been in vain. He is not able to bear the agony of watching the fanfare around the top guy. "My goal is to push the 1st ranking student from a top floor so that he falls down, gets a fracture and fails. I will then be the topper of the class". Negative.

This is like installing time bombs in your own home. Detonate those kinds of destructive goals.

There are two types of animals in the mind – a good animal and a bad animal. You will inhabit the character of the one you feed more during most part of the day.

It is advisable for Sumit to have a constructive goal such as, "I will sharpen my skills by learning the tools in the book named "Six Secrets Smart Students Don't Tell You", and implement its principles by studying for 3 hours daily".

Compare yourself against the goal, not people.

P – Practical:

Rahul says, "I am a 38% scoring student. I want to score 99% marks in the exam scheduled next month". Impractical. If this was possible, a donkey could become a horse in a day. Understanding reality is as important as having a nib in a pen.

Now a 38% scoring student should keep a first target of fetching 55% in his next exam. When the target is reached, the goal post must be extended to 65%, 80%, 85% and so on, in the subsequent exams. Aiming at an impractical goal will only disappoint you.

Rahul can have his goal as – "My last score was 38%. However, in the exam scheduled 30 days from now, I will score 55% by studying for 3 hours every day". This is a better goal.

The goal must be practical and should match your potential. Otherwise, it tends to become a castle in the air.

A – Arithmetical:

Do we go to a bazaar and ask for "some rice"? Rather, we ask for, say, ten kilograms of Basmati rice. Measurable. Arithmetical.

60% of goal setters start with the wrong personal goal, stating maybe – "I will become a good citizen this year". Instead, he might turn into a philosopher!

If your goal is not arithmetic, you are missing out on the equation.

T – Time bound:

"Until we manage time, we manage nothing." – Peter F Drucker

Don't you feel that the major chunk of our life is bound by time?

Right from our time in the womb, a class, a chemical reaction, the popularity of a gadget, the taste of food, a football match, infatuation, till the life span of a human being.

To simplify, if any goal doesn't have a time frame, it is bound to get diluted with time.

The best example is a 'New Year Resolution'. Come Jan 1st, robust aunties want to transform into a chiseled size zero, chain smoking uncles aim to shed their bad habit for their kid, tense businessmen want to cool down through meditation, we students dream of turning class toppers, and so on.

Utter failure. We deviate after a week. We turn – '*Chalta hai*'.

Reason? The goals are not time bound.

Suhas, a 16 year old, has a goal – "I want to learn playing the *Tabla*, from Guru Govind, and pass the junior exam." When? After his retirement?

The result will be postponement and failure. A timeframe is as important as the heart in us *homo sapiens*.

E – Elastic:

Goals are meant to be rigid and non-flexible. If we can change them, why have goals at all? – If this is your thought process, think again.

Payal, a 12th standard student in 2005 aspired to become a software engineer in a multinational company. She was about to opt for the IT stream in the entrance counselling the next day. Meanwhile, the software market seemed to be volatile, recession had spread, and jobs were as rare as an oasis in the Sahara desert. The situation was predicted to further worsen.

Should she still take her chances by choosing the software industry at such a pivotal time? Should she still stick to her 5 year old plan?

If yes, she might be making a blunder.

Alternatively, she can look into the courses which are on the verge of a boom and have the capability to make it big in the coming years.

Payal chose Biotechnology. She now works for a pharmaceutical company in Canada. If she had kept her previous goal rigid, her success would have been debatable.

Times change, markets change and amidst these changes, our goals ought to be flexible.

I – Individual:

"You must be the change you want to see in the world." – M.K Gandhi

Smith has an unusual goal – "My younger brother must get into the state-level cricket competition this year".

Rather, this should be Smith's brother's goal.

Any goal ought to be in your purview. You must be at the centre point of your goal circle. It must be personal and individual.

Smith's goal is positive; however, it mainly depends on someone else's effort and talent. Smith's personal scope in this context is limited.

Preferably, the same intent can be reached by modifying his point of view as follows: "Each day starting from tomorrow, I will wake my brother up at 5:30am so that he can attend his cricket practice on time."

The goal must say what you are supposed to do. The more the details, the more the efficiency.

What Next?

The Goals must be segregated into 4 timelines: 5 years, 1 year, 6 month, and 1 month goals. The last 3 timelines must contribute towards the 5 year goal.

Suppose your 5 year goal is to bake a 2 kg chocolate cake, then your 1 month goal must be to, say, collect 200gms of cocoa powder. The aim is to set your preferable big picture in the mind, and work towards it, in increments.

The Aim-Load-Shoot tool is given below.

Load-Aim-Shoot Tool			
Follow **Chennai Police ATE Ice cream** rule & Stretch your Creativity			
5- Year Goals	Priority	1- Year Goals	Priority
a)			
b)			
c)			
d)			
6- Months Goals	Priority	1- Month Goals	Priority
a)			
b)			
c)			
d)			
Prioritize into A, B and C			
A - Must Do B - Desirable to Do C - Can Wait			

My Present Absolute Important Goals are (Jot down all the "A" Priority goals into this list)	
Goals	Period

An example of a filled tool is as below:

Load-Aim-Shoot Tool			
Follow **Chennai Police ATE Ice cream** rule & Stretch your Creativity			
5- Year Goals	Priority	1- Year Goals	Priority
a) Finish Electronic Engg in RV College Bangalore in 2018 with 85% aggregate by studying smart for 3 hours every day.	A	a) Save 30 rupees every day to buy Firefox Mountaineering cycle on 12th Dec 2014	A
		b) Wake brother up at 6:00 am everyday so that he attends swimming coaching on time	B
b) Obtain "Rajyapuraskara" award with 80% in Scouts by attending the camp every Wednesday and Thursday in the institution.	B	c) Pass 12th Standard with 85% by following the six secrets and practising it for 3 hours each day	A
6- Months Goals	Priority	1- Month Goals	Priority
a) Reduce mom's work by cleaning my wardrobe on Sunday and washing plates and tumblers I use for eating: trial for 6 months	B	a) Patiently listen to grandma's boring flashbacks for 30 minutes and not doze off: trial for 1 month	C
b) Lose 5 kgs as per my Body mass index by Jogging with father from 6:30am-7:30 am	A	b) Solve Maths problems for 1 hour each day, study remaining 5 subjects taking one a day, so as to score 85% in unit test scheduled 28 days from now.	B

Prioritize into A, B and C	
A - Must Do B - Desirable to Do C - Can Wait	
My Present Absolute Important Goals are (Jot down all the "A" Priority goals into this list)	
Goals	Period
Electronic Engg - RV College - 85% - 3 hrs. study	5-Year
Save 30 rupees - everyday - Firefox cycle	1-Year
12th Std - 85% - Six secrets from this book	1-Year
Lose 5 kg - BMI - Jogging with father - 6:30-7:30 am	6-Month

***

"And don't forget to stick this sheet on the mirror in your room. I know you spend most of your time in front of it." Vimal said, pointing at the goal sheet I had just written down.

"Ya ya, thanks buddy," I said. My stomach juices were making merry in my tummy while he was burping.

"No-no, don't stare at me like that, see – I have kept this big piece of *Channa Batura* just for you!" he exclaimed.

I gobbled it up as though this was the last piece of food on earth. He cared. It showed.

Coincidently, the bell rang. Lunch break was done. Our class-mates came rushing back to reclaim their seats.

And yes, I had a secret to ponder.

***

Chapter Four:

Secret #2: Peacock with Two Chairs

"You can't wait for inspiration. You have to go after it with a club."

–Jack London

The amount of concentration a student has in the last period on a Saturday is the same as our interest in a Bangladesh vs. Canada cricket series. And God forbid, if it is a Social Studies lecture by Mr. Govind, the pace of your watch's needle will lose even against a snail.

Mr. Govind was well known as 'Drilling Govinda', thanks to his crazy habit of drilling his little finger into either his nose or ears. Post drilling session, he would smell the sticky substance clinging to the finger! This act had pushed him far away from the lady teachers, though he was strong in academics. However, his strictness stopped us from making fun of him in public.

Me and my bench mate Shamika were fond of the 'pen-fight' game. Your childhood is incomplete if you missed out on that game, where you use your pens like a carrom striker on the desk to eliminate the opponent. As competition in the class was tough, I was using a heavy metal fountain pen as my weapon.

"Are you thinking what I am thinking?" she asked me. Our thoughts always synchronised, but I didn't want to take the chance of playing the game in this class because:

- If a teacher punishes you on a Saturday, your whole Sunday seems like a flop movie.
- This was Drilling Govinda's class, he was strict, and we were sitting on the third bench – where he had a commanding view.
- By chance if I got caught and he slapped me, the sticky thing from his little finger would get transferred to my cheeks! Why take risks?

Shamika was the cutest girl of the class and many boys had crossed swords with me as I was her best friend. I would always dress neatly only because she would sit beside me.

No, our behaviour, tastes and outlook didn't match:

- She is a genius – a topper, but I am an average student (sometimes below average).
- She is neat, organized, keeps things tidy; I am sloppy, disorganised and dirty (always).
- She is pretty and I am not handsome (no grace marks here).
- She likes South Indian food and I love North Indian cuisine.
- She is sentimental. I am also sentimental (Oh! At last one thing matches).
- Why am I saying all this?

"Only one game, come on!" she insisted and placed her Reynolds pen on the desk, and raised her eyebrows expecting me to do the same.

Two things tempted me:

1. Her winning percentage was high in our battles. But this time she had a lighter pen, and my chances of winning were good.

2. Her mesmerising eyes were hypnotising me, though I tried my best to avoid eye contact.

"Ok, only one game!" I said, raising my forefinger firmly. I couldn't decline.

As soon as I took my first shot, the lecture paused for a few seconds. Before I even realised the unusual calmness in the class, a chalk-piece struck my head sharply from nowhere!

It was Mr. Govind who had thrown his chalk!

The class turned pin drop silent. I stood up in despair. He was angry that I had dared to play in HIS class. The 1 rupee coin size black mole on his cheek made him look even fiercer.

Shamika stood up as well, acknowledging her participation.

"You both get *aauut aaf mai claas*" he ordered. Giggles sprouted in the class. "*Anybady waants* to *jaain them*?" he continued, in typical teacher style, as the giggles gradually dissolved. Everybody wanted to escape, but the problem is, democracy doesn't work in a class.

I wished I could take my bag along, as this was the last class of the week. But I feared his little finger.

We moved slowly towards the exit which was 5 rows away! More time for my classmates to look at us, sympathise and feel proud that THEY were not punished. A few last bench students stared at us till we disappeared from their sight.

We both stood in an area blind to Mr. Govind.

"It's all because of me, I am sorry!" Shamika started sobbing. She was a usual customer in the top 5 ranks, and students of that calibre have SERIOUS trouble facing criticism; completely opposite to me.

"I should help you in some way, else I will always be sorry for this," her sobs deepened.

The school clerk passing by in the corridor kept staring at me as though I was the one making her cry!

Her sobbing rose from *Volume 10* to *Volume 50* in a few seconds. If the Volume turned around 55 or more, she would be audible to the class. It was at a threshold point. I wished I had a remote which could *mute* her.

Girls are so strange!

"Chill, chill, chill, you will help me, I will help you to do that," I even had to negotiate. Boy, what a life!

"Tell me the secret of your good scores. You always outsmart the cream of the class. How do you manage to do it each time?"

I asked her straight.

This statement of mine automatically muted her for a while. I needed an answer. I suppose that was a big question compared to the favour she offered.

"Can you come to my home this evening for a cup of coffee? Today was a messy day!" she said after thinking.

The bell rang. We had to collect our bags and part ways.

"No probs, it's fine, see you on Monday then, bye," I said. She was conservative; I suppose, she didn't want to share.

"My secret is in my home. I can tell you only if you come home. I will be waiting at 6:30pm for you," she said, winked, and disappeared into the crowd.

What a twist! As I said, girls are strange.

***

What do you get by walking east from my home for 20 minutes?

Shamika's home!

I was nervous as this was the first time I had visited a girl's place. I stood there sharp at 6:30pm with a *Dairy Milk* chocolate in hand, as I was scared to go empty-handed.

As soon as the door opened, I gave her the chocolate – which seemed like a 'you-had-forgotten-this-thing-so-I-came-to-return-it' kind of act! Shamika and her mom welcomed me warmly. She took the chocolate with a girly, "Awwww", and her mom served lime juice. They were a middle class family and their home was a bit smaller than ours, but clean and tidy.

When all our smiles felt stretched and artificial, Shamika broke the silence: "Come, I'll show you my room!"

The door of her room had a sign board:

> ## Peacock With Two Chairs
> ### Trespassers Will Be Prosecuted!

When she opened the door, I was instantly star struck looking around the walls of her room where flip charts were embalmed, posters were glued, marks cards were affixed, frames were hooked, a mini rocket was painted, flow charts were drawn, and so on! There was limited space on the walls and ceiling. But it neither seemed over-populated nor a waste of time. It was motivating, artistic and out of the box. The whole room was colourful, completely contrary to the remaining areas of the house.

There was a single bed, a study table, a small wardrobe; and 2 chairs – each facing different walls – a little weird.

Shamika smiled and was proudly showcasing her room.

"This is my secret laboratory," she said.

***

Scene 1: Your mom prepares a cabbage-turnip-beetroot salad, gives you a 'but-its-healthy-dear' look, serves it on a steel plate and forces you to eat it.

Do you feel like savouring it? You will definitely stick out your tongue and silently push off from the dining table.

Scene 2: Using the same cabbage-turnip-beetroot salad, your mom prepares a pizza, lays it out on a decorative glass plate, artistically squeezes some tomato ketchup over it and rings the dinner bell. Will you eat it?

I challenge you that you will chomp it up even if you are full. Why would you miss such a gourmet dish?

Our moods and behaviour are directly proportional to the surroundings. For instance, when you go to a temple, your mind relaxes. You go to an amusement park, your mind changes gear to enjoyment. You go to your relatives' home; you become so decent that your father gets confused. You don't bargain at a mall, but fight for a 50% discount from a street vendor. You become all 'proper' in an airplane and turn local in a train. You frown while looking at your present school/college, whereas a glimpse at the movie theatre makes you glad.

> ## The atmosphere you live in, influences 70% of your decisions, behaviour and character!

This is one of the reasons why institutions force their students to dress in uniforms; professionals gear-up in formals, businessmen flaunt suits, and doctors wear lab coats or scrubs.

Furthermore, nature itself manipulates the attributes of creatures in relation to their environments. A polar bear – owing to the chilly weather at the poles – has a 3-inch thick skin. Many animals hibernate in the winter. Trees shed leaves in autumn and grow new ones in spring.

A common story parents/grand-parents tell, is of the 'twin parrots'. One parrot was adopted by a butcher, the other by a saint. With time, their speech was influenced by their masters and surroundings; and the attitude of the parrots grew poles apart.

Examples can go on for pages, but the conclusion is simple: The atmosphere you live in will influence the results.

No matter how big or small your house is, whether you have a separate room or not, you are rich or poor, it is YOUR responsibility to create an environment conductive to studying. YOU are the creator of the aura around you.

Let me re-emphasise: 70% of your results depend upon the ambience you create around you.

Here are the 6 rules to ensure a constructive study space:

> **Rule 1:** Sparkle Shine
>
> **Rule 2:** Radar Range
>
> **Rule 3:** Right-click re-load
>
> **Rule 4:** Yogananda
>
> **Rule 5:** Peacock
>
> **Rule 6:** 2-chair technique

Rule 1: Sparkle shine

George, a 2nd year B.Com student studies in a place full of old underwear, antique dust, ink blotches on the floor resembling an ancient map, sharpener dust of the last 6 months, gum smeared on the desk, a glass of cold milk with a mosquito swimming calmly on it, scratched DVDs all over the place, passport size photos of deities scattered, a fan full of spider webs; Boroplus, Burnol, Crocin; pieces of roti fallen all over. What a serene, sterilised place!

Though the situation had gone to the dogs, he managed to look at the mirror and smile!

If this scene resembles your study area, it is time to change. Keep your room/study place neat and tidy. Let it be free of everything else. Do not keep anything around except organised study materials.

Ensure that you study in the same place and don't change your spot often.

Let the place be free from any bad odour. If needed, spray room freshener or light an incense stick. Open the windows for light and fresh air to cleanse the place.

> # Your Room Is The Reflection Of Your Mind!
> # Let It Sparkle Shine!

Rule 2: Radar Range

Shweta has her pencil on the desk, eraser in the bag, graph sheets in the wardrobe. She wants to study Biology, but the text book is in the living room!

She gets up and goes to collect it, but thanks to her brother who is watching her favourite programme on TV, she can't stop herself from watching it. And yes, the biology unit test goes for a toss the next day.

This scenario can be avoided if the required materials of study such as geometric instruments, pen/pencil, calculator, bag, text books, etc. are in your radar range.

Before a study session begins, quickly double check availability. *Plus, ensure you don't waste more time arranging the necessities.* This generally is a standard deviation from study-time.

There are instances when you sit down to study, realise that you don't have some stationery, say, a black ink pen and you run to the nearest store to get it. On the way, a friend of yours diverts you to the nearest *pani-puri* stall instead.

Follow a simple rule to avoid this:

> # If Your Study Materials Are Not Within Reach,
> # The Deviations Will Be!

Rule 3: Right-click–Reload

Google chrome – Facebook-Login – Status update as – 'Boring to study' – wait for likes and comments – minimize (Oh no! Mom came) – "Ma, I am working on a project, don't disturb me now, ok

I'll drink milk" – Thank god – Maximize – Wow! One 'like' from Priyanka – One 'comment' from Yousuf – right-click – reload.

In parallel, chat on mobile: *Hi wt r u doin?–Nothin Dude prparin fo d test–hw many units done?–Me zero, you hero!*

Simultaneously you are reading: *the unit on Electromagnetism, the whole chapter extends for 32 pages!*

iPod is playing 'Gangnam Style' in the background; and you have a new notification on Facebook...

You may be a 21st century gadget guru, you may tease your parents when they are unable to send a simple message from the mobile, you may be a hero/heroine in your neighbourhood, you may be the best problem solver to your friend, and you may have the costliest and latest gadgets at home. But, if your studying time resembles the above drama, cut it out. Stop it now!

When it comes to acquiring knowledge, the human brain is not built to multi-task. It takes time to shift your attention back to study. So, switch off and ban those diversions from your study place.

Make your study time 'no-gadget' time.

If you lack self control, tell your parent/guardian to sit with you when you are studying; this will force you to refrain from these activities.

> **If You Indulge In *Right-Click–Reload* During Study Time, Your Results Will *Right-Click–Refresh* Your Academic Year.**

Rule 4: Yogananda

My friend Babu does Yoga during studies.

Step 1: *Sit with a book on the bed. Feel comfortable; adjust your posture if required. Take deep breaths.*

Step 2: *Slowly extend your legs, scratch your stomach; curse your teacher and university for introducing such a subject.*

Step 3: *Lie down completely, let the book rest on the pillow and you rest on the bed. If anybody complains that you are not studying, show them the book; stare at the book till they get out of the room.*

Step 4: *Closing the eyelids feels like heaven. Try it. A few seconds later, a dog barks and wakes you up. Curse the dog; resume staring at the book for few more minutes.*

Step 5: *Realise that closing the eyelids was not a bad idea at all. Postpone study time by 1 hour to round-off. Close your eye lids again to doze off.*

There is a huge difference between a *comfortable* position and a *cozy* position. One will let you study; the other will encourage you to sleep.

The body's habit when lying down is to relax and sleep. Why should we fight that tendency? In addition, lying down promotes passive reading and it is hard to take notes or type while lying down. So, students who study lying down are playing a less active role in their learning than those who study sitting up.

Sit on a stiff chair and never on the bed or sofa. Don't let the angle of view strain your eyes.

Studying On a Sofa or a Bed
Will Make Johnny's Concentration Dead

Rule 5: Peacock

Suhas is an entrepreneur. He has a start-up company which was not making any profits in 2003. However, he was determined to make *a mark and earn at least $20 million by 2010. He tore a cheque leaf from his account and wrote '$20000000' on it, payable to 'Self'. He then stuck it on the ceiling of his room such that whenever he lay on his bed, he could see the cheque.*

7 years later, guess what, he had earned $22.6 million. More than his ambition!

Colourful, positive and stimulating affirmations around you provide you a direct flight ticket from where-you-are to where-you-want-to-be.

Make your room a masterpiece. Drown yourself with creative placards, pictures and slogans; so much, that you have no time and space for negative thoughts.

You can also paste few formulae. Ensure that only important formulae are put up, and not the whole text book.

Change the position of the hung pictures once in a fortnight. Add new affirmations and delete old ones from the wall once in a month. Else, these will be new homes for spiders!

Till You Colour Your World, It Will Remain Dark!

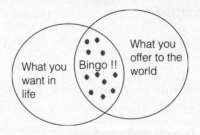

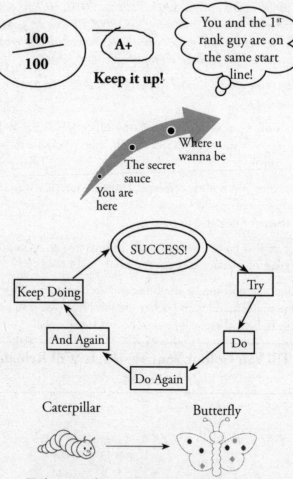

Today may be a testing time, but after I surpass this, life is colourful!

<u>Rule 6:</u> The Two Chair Technique

In the USA, most families have 2 cars. One could be for the office on weekdays, the other for picnics on weekends. The weekday car is usually a sedan – which gives you a professional look, whereas, the weekend one is an MUV/SUV which can accommodate family members and luggage for a long journey.

Involuntarily, the mood and the mindset change with the car you sit in.

Similarly, we students must have two chairs for studies. One chair for reading/comprehending the chapters, called the *'reading chair'*. A table can be used to support your study materials. All the reading, problem-solving, etc. must happen when you are sitting on this chair, facing the wall.

The other must be the *'recall chair',* where you recall what you have just read. This chair must be placed facing a different wall than that of the *reading chair*.

For every one hour of studying, five minutes of recollection is recommended. This process is done by closing the eyes, picturing each sheet you read/solved. A rough sheet can also be used, if necessary.

> ## The Two Chair Technique Helps In Winning Your Dream Seat!

If these 6 rules are implemented, a huge change can be seen right from the next exam!

***

My bonding with and respect towards Shamika quadrupled after that meeting. Our eyes met and I wanted to thank her.

"Ok, you are welcome," she smiled. I told you, our thoughts synchronise.

It was 7:30pm already. My father would be home by then.

Ours is an orthodox family. If my brother or I entered home after HE entered, we would be scrutinised and questioned intensely. The reason for being late had to be confidently uttered and had to seem realistic. If we stammered or showed any signs of lying, dinner time would be pure torture! And what would happen if I said, "I am late because I was at a girl's house?"

Very simple, I would be thrown out of both family photo and family tree.

"Aunty, thanks for the juice, Shamika, come home sometime. Happy weekend," I said. I wanted to disappear and fast!

"Will you not invite *me* to your home?" her mom asked. All aunties have trademarked formalities and time-wasting techniques for good-for-nothing chatting, that too when you are in a hurry.

I laughed as though she had cracked a joke, and skedaddled.

Shamika kept waving her hand till we were out of sight of each other.

What a day! Playing in Drilling Govinda's class, getting punished with Shamika, and as a bonus point, visiting her room as well!

I couldn't have slept that night even if I had gulped sleeping pills.

And how did my father welcome me home that night? Censor cut!

***

Chapter Five:

Secret #3: A 500 Page Book – On The Tip of Your Tongue

"The best revenge is massive success."

–Frank Sinatra

We often tend to open the fridge although we know there is nothing to eat. Similarly, teachers ask questions to the class though they know that the students can't answer them.

"*Waat ees tha faarmula aaf* (a-b) whole cube? Chandan, *kyan* you *answar*?" Mrs. Sunitha asked me.

I didn't know the answer. The lady who made my mom cry during the recent parent-teacher meeting was resuming her torture.

After a long pause, she made a long face as she knew I couldn't answer, and turned to Ravi – a brighter bulb of the class. "Ravi, can you answer this basic question please?"

He answered.

"You" she pointed at me, "at *leest repeet waat* he said, *noo!*" She taunted me.

Frankly speaking, I had not listened to Ravi's answer, as my mind was busy in rewinding the tape of her behaviour during the horrendous parent-teacher debacle.

"Ah, *avar innoocent* butterfly *ees waandering aan* a *diffarent* planet," she said and signalled Ravi to repeat his answer.

This time I parroted his answer.

My vision at that moment turned blurry due to the tears in my eyes. I didn't want to blink. If I did, they would flow down my eyes. I felt ashamed.

If there were any discussions in class about probable exam result rankings, the 1st place was never discussed as Ravi was a fixture there. Not only Math, he was proficient in all subjects. When did *Lal*, *Bal* and *Pal* die? He had the date on his tongue. He could recite any poem from the curriculum as easily as our national anthem; he was able to reproduce the answers in the exam as it was in the text book. Plus, he would provide its page number accurately as if he was born to do that.

Earlier we felt that he was a master of some malpractice to score marks. But when his high scores became as regular as the rain in Cherapunji, we realized that this chap is smart and is doing things differently.

There is one 'Ravi' in each school and I wanted to know their secret.

I tore a small piece of paper from the last page of my Math notes, and wrote – 'I want to know your secret to studying, can you please tell me? I can offer you my lunch for a week in return, I promise.' As soon as Mrs. Sunitha turned towards the board to solve a problem, I crumpled the paper, signalled to Ravi and threw it at him.

He read it and immediately started writing on the other side of the chit. I was delighted. The secret was only a few seconds away!

He threw the chit, and I caught it as carefully as we catch a nugget of 24 carat gold. I held it under the desk so that nobody else got a glimpse of it other than me. It read – 'Hey dumbo, go get a life! ☺'.

I thought for a while, tore one more chit, and wrote – 'Thanks for your suggestion. I thought you would be interested to get *GTA Vice City* and *Age of Empires* limited edition games as well. It's ok, better luck next time.' And threw it at him. He was a maniac when it came to computer games, and his parents didn't buy him games thinking that it would bring his scores down.

I didn't have those games with me, but that was the only bait I could offer him. He took time to think about it, and replied – 'Let's discuss the secret this evening at your place, with the computer games.'

Wow! The fish was hooked. 'Great! And my mom was planning to prepare *chakkali* today!' I replied with another chit. Additional bait for safety!

This secret is one of the most productive of the lot.

***

"Use your brains! You sing film songs effortlessly and recite movie dialogues flawlessly; but can't you remember your notes and write the exam efficiently?" Joy's father would question Joy whenever he complained about his bad memory.

Was Joy's father right? Definitely YES!

Today, in the world of DVDs and blu-ray disks that can store reams of information and reproduce them at will, we forget things much too easily. We tend to limit our use of the most productive and efficient think-tank of our body – *the brain*.

> ## You Have Memory Problems Only If You Get Up In The Morning And Fail To Recall Your Own Name.

If Vijay needs a robot to utter every day, "Good Morning, your name is Vijay," only then does he have a bad memory. If you don't need such help, you can improve your ability to recall by a minimum of 400%, starting today!

There are instances when you may:

- Hear someone who is talking to you, but don't *listen* to them.
- Stare at a person for a long time, yet, do not *see* him/her.
- Inhale smoke, but do not *register* its smell.
- Touch an iron box by mistake, but do not *feel* it.
- Stare at a book for a long time but fail to *read* it.

These inconsistencies are due to the fog which is blocking your mind. The fog may comprise anger, pity, envy, grief, restlessness, lust, fear, depression, among many. These are factors which reduce your success rate.

If **Reading** and **Retention** are placed on two sides of a see-saw, see to it that it should not wobble.

Two steps are necessary in order to study smartly and memorize:

Step 1: *Remove those blocking fogs from your mind for the next 50 minutes.*

Step 2: *Think creatively/out-of-the-box to remember what you study.*

Many students complain that the Step 1 can somehow be done with great difficulty but not Step 2. However, here is a simple example which will prove otherwise:

If anybody asks you the direction of a place you are well aware of, you reply appropriately. Though you stand at a single spot while explaining to them, your mind creatively maps the source and the destination, and provides the appropriate route.

You have inbuilt creativity and imagination, but fail to exploit this trait.

Sanjeev's concept of studying was to understand the topic and try to reproduce his understanding on the exam sheet. However, the evaluator felt that the answer he wrote in the exam pertained to a different theory altogether! He might have written pages and pages, yet he scored low marks. The reason was, his answers missed the vital 'keywords'.

Each Chapter Is Divided Into Multiple Paragraphs. The Number Of Sentences In Each Paragraph Varies. One Paragraph May Have 10 Sentences; The Other May Have Just Two. Why?

One single paragraph will pertain to only one KEYWORD.

This *keyword* is then expanded, explained and exaggerated to form sentences and a paragraph. Hence, the number of sentences in each paragraph is unique.

If you are able to identify those *keywords* in each paragraph, map them, and recall them; you will then score marks!

The following 4 tools will help you remember the whole curriculum effectively and score well!

Tool 1: **Bedtime Stories**

Tool 2: **Let Us Have A Peg!**

Tool 3: **Rubber Band**

Tool 4: **Go Home**

Keyword > Association > Picture

Tool 1 – Bedtime Stories

Stories are the best mediums through which a person can comprehend concepts. We still remember the bedtime stories our parents/grand parents told us in our childhood because they were interesting and magical!

If we use the same story-telling techniques to study, the word 'examination' will sound merrier.

Example 1:

The following is an excerpt from a newspaper:

Govt. Set To Construct 10 New Airports

The government has decided to construct 10 new airports. The process will be kicked off in six major cities going for international bidding in the first phase. A meeting of an inter-ministerial group on this issue with representatives from Planning Commission, Finance, Law and Aviation ministries will be held on Thursday.

"These airports will be operated, managed and further developed by 2 special players." said a senior official of the aviation ministry.

When asked why the government is initiating this process with barely a few months to go for the polls, the official said: "The process is being started and we hope to put the blueprint in place. This takes time but we are doing the groundwork".

The places which were once a haven for goondas and bootleggers in metropolitan cities are being proposed as the areas for airports so as to minimise further deforestation in the country.

The opposition parties, on the other hand, are fuming. They say that the bathroom facilities in the country must be improved and the creation of posh airports should not be a priority.

Let us assume, in an exam, we are asked to write about the '10 new airports' for 10 marks.

To use the *Bedtime stories* tool, you need to:

- Identify the KEYWORD of each paragraph. Using this keyword, you should be able to develop the whole paragraph with ease.
- Concatenate the identified keywords from all the paragraphs to build your-own-creative-story which is not related to the subject! Create unrealistic characters and plots for better retention.

The keywords from the above excerpt could be:

1st paragraph: "**10 new airports**", 2nd paragraph: "**two special players**", 3rd paragraph: "**blueprint**", 4th paragraph: "**goonda and bootlegging people**", 5th paragraph: "**bathroom**".

The made-up weird story can be as below:

*Long ago, the **10 new airports** were being ruled by **two special players**. They had the **blueprint** of the airports, which was top secret. But one fine day, some **goondas and bootleggers** attacked them, stole the blueprint, and ran to the **bathroom**.*

Close your eyes and re-construct the storyline in motion.

During the exam you should be able to recall this story, identify the keywords, and describe them. The advantage is that you are less likely to miss out on the keywords!

That's 10 marks in your kitty!

Example 2:

The keywords in some other chapter are: **Forest, banana, blade, mobile phone, coffin, friend, explosion, cloud, buildings, gold coins, chocolate, statue, bus, and home.**

The tale can be on similar lines:

*Long ago, in a **forest** I found a **banana**. When I cut it using a **blade**, a **mobile phone** popped out of it! Adding to the surprise, it rang. The call was from a **coffin**! However, during the conversation we became **friends**. Suddenly, the mobile blew up in an **explosion**. The smoke created **clouds** which floated above many **buildings**. People started throwing **gold coins** and **chocolates** at the clouds. The **statue** which was witnessing all this, got up, boarded a **bus** and went **home**.*

> **If Four Important 10 Mark Answers Are Retained Using Stories, You Get A Cool 40 Marks Without Much Effort!**

If this tool is used appropriately, you will definitely score better. You can also use this method to memorize To-Do lists, routes, etc.

Tool 2: Let Us Have A Peg!

While ascending steep mountains, mountaineers find it hard to maintain support and balance. They are prone to slip, lose their grip and fall during a climb. Hence they use a *peg* – a sharp nail-like metal piece which is hammered onto the surface of the hill to climb comfortably while taking its support.

Similarly, we students are prone to forgetting and can turn blank in exam halls. This pegging tool will assist us in overcoming these limitations.

Associations are an integral part of our life. When we hear a song sung by Sonu Nigaam, we immediately associate the voice with his physical appearance. As soon as you hear somebody saying '*Gulab Jamun*', you imagine the sweet and your mouth starts watering. We are able to come home each day from work/educational institution, because of our mind's association with the route.

On the whole, our subconscious mind has a specific association for every object or feeling in this world. If this basic instinct is capitalised upon in a smart way, it can help us in our studies.

To use this tool, you need to:

- Have a specific and definite '*peg*' with numbers. That is, your mind must record one single object for one specific number. When you are asked about the number, the corresponding object must be uttered immediately and vice versa. Eg: I use 'auto rickshaw' as the peg for the number '3'. (As the auto rickshaw has 3 wheels, pegging it with the number '3' makes sense)
- Use the defined peg to *associate* reactively with the *keyword*. E.g.: if the third *keyword* in a chapter is *a cow*, I imagine that *a cow* is riding the *auto rickshaw*! (As auto rickshaw is my peg for number 3).
- Similarly associate all *key points* with their own pegs and recall in any order.

The following can be a *peg* for the corresponding numbers:

Number 1: Lamppost (the number one looks like a pole, a lamppost can act as a peg for it. A lamppost is also known as a street light).

Number 2: Knee Joint (as there are only two knee joints in a human body, we can use this as a peg for the number 2).

Number 3: Auto-Rickshaw (as these are three wheelers).

Number 4: Car (four wheelers, an easy peg for the number 4).

Number 5: Five star chocolate (self explanatory).

Number 6: Sixer (easy to remember for boys).

Number 7: 7'O clock shaving blade (you can also use 'a week' as a peg).

Number 8: Octopus (owing to its eight tentacles).

Number 9: Gems (dedicated to 'Navaratna' in Sanskrit).

Number 10: Fingers (exception if you are Hrithik Roshan who has 11 fingers).

This is a sample of 10 pegs. You can extend the method till you have constructed an ideal 50 *pegs*.

For instance, let us associate pegs with the following 10 keywords from an excerpt :1) **Tie, 2) Remote, 3) Cow, 4) Water, 5) Iron, 6) Apple, 7) Leather, 8) Computer, 9) Countries, 10) Hair.**

The association of the peg with these keywords can be as follows.

Number 1: Imagine that you are tying the **Tie** to the **Lamp Post.**

Number 2: Visualise that you are pressing the **Remote** buttons with your **knee joints!**

Number 3: Dream that a **cow** is driving the **auto rickshaw,** and is beating the traffic easily.

Number 4: A **car** is being driven on **water**!

Number 5: **Five star chocolate** is made of **iron** and you are trying to eat it!

Number 6: You are hitting **apples** for **sixes** instead of the ball.

Number 7: Imagine that you are shaving the **leather** piece using the **7'O clock shaving blade**!

Number 8: The **octopus** uses its tentacles to use the **computer**.

Number 9: Gems are thrown up high and land on all the **countries** of the world.

Number 10: Visualize that **hair** is growing densely all over your **fingers**!

This tool can be used to remember bullet point answers, or to answer '*advantages/disadvantages*' and '*differences between*' questions.

Have a peg each day!

Tool 3: Rubber Band

What are the colours of the rainbow? Even a primary school student can answer this with ease – VIBGYOR – **V**iolet **I**ndigo **B**lue **G**reen **Y**ellow **O**range and **R**ed!

This is a tool we use from our childhood and is known as an *Acronym*.

Forming an acronym is a great strategy to use and remember information in any order. An acronym is a word that is formed from the first letter of each keyword to be remembered. It can form a real word or a sentence is formed using those first letters.

For electronic engineering students, **B.B. ROY Of Great Britain** has a **Very Good Wife: BBROYGBVGW** – is an acronym used to find the resistor colour code.

Biology students use a simple acronym to remember the stages of cell division – **I**van **P**urchased a **MAT: I**nterphase, **P**rophase, **M**etaphase, **A**naphase, and **T**elephase

Math equations are solved using a simple sequence: **P**lease **E**xc use **M**y **D**ear **A**unt **S**ally – PEMDAS: **P**arenthesis, **E**xponents, **M**ultiplication, **D**ivision, **A**ddition, **S**ubtraction!

The goal-setting technique was explained in Chapter 3 using an acronym: **C**hennai **P**olice **ATE I**ce-cream, which expands as **C**onstructive, **P**ractical, **A**rithmetical, **T**ime bound, **E**lastic, and **I**ndividual.

Srikanth cannot seem to remember the 6 Noble gases. The rubber band tool can help him out!

The 6 noble gases are: **He**lium, **Ne**on, **Ar**gon, **Kr**ypton, **Xe**non and **Ra**don.

He-man Ran to Krishh's house and Nearly killed him with an aXe!

Even in his sleep, Srikanth can now recall all the noble gases!

Tool 4: Go Home

Kalpesh studies mechanical engineering. He remembers his route from his college to home like the back of his hand. Such is the relationship you form with the route you have taken for a long time.

He wrote down all the landmarks in the route:

College ➔ **Bapu CIRCLE** ➔ **Kapu Police Station** ➔ **Rajput Water TANK** ➔ **Poorna Layout** ➔ **Gurukul BUS DEPOT** ➔ **Sai BABA TEMPLE** ➔ **Home**

Now, he can use these landmarks and associate them with the keywords. Recalling them will be as simple as drinking water!

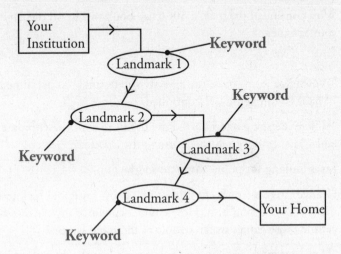

Similarly, the route from your *best friend's home* to your *home;* or the way from *your college* to the nearest *movie theatre* (this is easily recallable!), can be used for different associations in different subjects/chapters.

Note:

- You need to keep your pegs/landmarks/acronyms constant. Say, the peg for number 2 is *knee joints*; it should not change to *eyes* the next day.
- Your memory is as volatile as that of Aamir Khan in *Ghajini*; hence these pegs/landmarks can be re-used for different keywords after a few days.
- Let the association be dynamic and creative. If the sequence imagined is something normal like – *the sun sets in the west,* you are bound to forget as easily as a husband forgetting his wife's birthday!

If all these four tools are used judiciously, you will be able to remember and recall many chapters.

With continued practice, a 500-page book will be on the tip of your tongue!

***

"Wow! We can make studies so interesting!" I exclaimed. "Thanks a lot, genius," I continued.

"Where are the game CDs?" Ravi began to scan the computer table. His teeth were busy churning the *chakkali*.

I was looking for polite words to soothe him.

His eyes were as innocent as that of a baby. Little did he know that I was cheating him! How could I convince my parents to get me those games worth couple of thousand rupees?

"Hey, I forgot to tell you, my father has taken the CDs to office today; I will surely give them to you tomorrow," I lied. *Even imagining my father playing computer games at his office was so amusing!*

He returned home empty handed but with a full stomach.

The next day I bought him those games. There went my piggy bank and six months' savings, in lieu of increasing my knowledge bank.

He was delighted and gave me a *I-knew-it* expression. I suppose he had believed that my father plays computer games at his office!

***

Chapter Six:

Secret #4: Tuition Fees in the Bank

"If you don't run your own life, somebody else will."

—John Atkinson

Come January, an election-like atmosphere is created in and around a 5 kilometre radius of every educational institution. The reason: the marketing campaigns of tutorials for the *next* academic year!

Tutorials are extra-coaching centres which match with a college/school, similar to SIM cards merging with mobile phones. If you are not admitted to one, you will be an outcaste!

By the time the school bell rings at 5:00pm, there will be competition between parents and flyer distributors on who will reach the kid first. In most cases, the latter have an upper hand.

Parents follow the flowchart below to decide if their kid needs to join a tutorial.

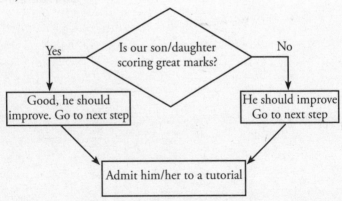

We students judge a tutorial based on the following parameters and in the same order of priority:

- Freebies if any: *One tutorial announced that they would give away bags and Parker pens for the first 25 joiners!*
- Proximity to home: *Maximum points if very near, as we can sleep more and still arrive* on time *for early morning classes.*
- Reviews from a senior or friend, plus overall credibility of the tutorial.

- Graphic design and photos on the flyer: *More graphics, more points. If it has pretty girls in it, double points.*
- Number of toppers and their marks: *Points increase three-fold if it has more boys with good marks. Girls study better anyway; the challenge is in making boys score more!*

It's a very simple selection process! We judge the tutorials based on the above points and shortlist the ones which score greater than our defined 'cut off'. Later, we join the one which charges the least among them.

Informal debate competitions take place among classmates, defending their choice of tutorial. Sometimes the debate turns so intense that it ends in scuffles and bloodshed!

Aniruddha, an average student of our class had chosen *Bhavathi Tutorial*. It was one of the costliest tutorials in south Bangalore and his parents could afford the fees of 1 lakh for his 10th standard tutorial alone! *That is more than the yearly salary of approximately 70% of employees in India.* The disgusting part was that, he was looked upon as the 'King of the Class' only because he had joined that tutorial!

Sridhar on the other hand was a non controversial top-ranking student and was in the good books of the class. He was strictly against the tutorial system and diplomatically condemned the practice.

Unfortunately, Aniruddha and Sridhar were bench mates, who were seated in front of me.

It was a free period. Sridhar and I casually started a conversation.

"Any plans of breaking your jinx and joining a tutorial? 10th standard could be our turning point!" I winked at him.

"Tuitions are a waste of time and money. I wonder why people don't use their brains," he ridiculed Aniruddha, infuriating him.

"You say I don't use my brains? Damn you!" Aniruddha echoed this sentence several times, tightened his fists and started wrestling with Sridhar! It turned so violent that Sridhar's mouth started to bleed.

We boys can get really worked up about small hurts to our ego and similar issues. A few classmates and I had to physically try our might to break-up the fight.

When the whole world is okay with tutorials, when the educational institutions themselves suggest tutorials to students, when society outlaws you if you do not attend a tutorial, here is a gentleman whose thought process was vertically opposite! I wanted to have a one-on-one conversation with this brave soul. What was he doing that others were not and yet how did he score better marks?

After the conflict calmed, I asked him, "What's your problem?"

The answer he provided was jaw dropping.

***

Statistics say that the below are the common (unconscious) reasons why students attend tutorials:

- My father bought me a new bike. I can't ride it to school, so let me take it to tutorials to show off.
- I can't wear tight t-shirts and low-waist jeans to college, however, no dress code in tutorials. Great hangout!
- Let me listen to the lecture in the tutorials so that I can sleep in college.
- I don't know what else to do in the evening. Attending tutorials is not a bad idea!
- I attend only because my crush attends the same tutorials.
- My college lecturers are good for nothing; paying high tuition fees may result in good lectures.

- All my friends are attending. People wouldn't have joined if it was good for nothing. Let me join as well.

Out of all those reasons, 80% of students fall into the 'tutorial trap' for the last reason alone!

On the flipside, parents have a different set of reasons to push their kid into tutorials:

- I want my child to be busy 24/7. I don't want him to waste time.
- Going to tutorials makes my son /daughter sharp.
- I can save income tax by spending on my child's tutorials! A win-win situation!
- I can boast at my 'kitty party' about my son's admission to the costliest tutorials in town!
- What if my son /daughter fails by not going to tutorials?
- All the kids in the neighbourhood attend! I need to send my child as well; the competition is cut-throat. Why should my child be left out?

Astonishingly, 95% of parents bravely admit that the last reason affects them the most.

To summarise, we all join these tutorials and waste time and money, only because we don't want to be separated from the herd. We want to be one amongst many. We feel 'left out of the tribe' if we do things others don't do. We don't want to stand out. We don't look for alternatives to study and score marks.

We are taught to be afraid!

We are brought up in a fear-filled atmosphere. People scare us and we are made to fear. This concept may seem a bit confusing, but it is justified. Let me explain:

'Fear' has long been the garnish in the sweet dish named 'child-hood'. There are many such instances in our childhood. Say—

- Eat properly or else a GHOST will haunt you.
- Come 'in time' to class, else you will get a RED mark and will be suspended.
- Sit quietly or you will be THROWN OUT of the class and we will inform your parents.
- Drink milk or your father will SLAP you.
- Finish your homework or you will become a BEGGAR and/or go to the dogs.

This is the way we are brought up, unfortunately. This is the way we grow up and shape our future. And the legacy continues from one generation to the other.

> Fear makes people go nuts. People take a *life insurance policy* amounting to 40–50% of their salary! It is so pitiful to see their predicament due to the fear of untimely death. People spend on an average ₹20,000 rupees to buy *Reverse Osmosis filter systems*, though their tap water is tested and found to be soft and pure!
>
> ***And similarly, we fear getting fewer marks, so we join a tutorial – whether it's helpful or not.***

On an average, a tutorial has 40-50 students jam-packed in a class, teaching the same old syllabus which is taught in the school/college; in a similar 'one-to-many' format, in a comparably boring fashion and an identical stinky atmosphere!

Let us calculate the time and money spent on joining a tutorial:

Time:

Total time in a day: 24 hours

Sleep: 8 to 9 hours. Guys like me utilise 10 hours (+ 2 to 3 hrs sleep in the class). Never mind, let us consider 8 hours.

Ablutions, Make-Up, Getting Ready: 1 hour for boys, 3 hours for girls. Consider the minimum − 1 hour.

School/College: 9 hours. Even if we bunk all the classes, we'll sincerely go home only at the regular timings, but that's a different story. So let us consider 9 hours.

Breakfast, Dinner, Parents Scolding: 1.5 hours. If watching TV simultaneously, 3 hours. But for calculation's sake, consider 1.5 hours.

Travel: The country's revenue can be guessed, but due to traffic, you can't predict the time required to reach the nearest supermarket. There goes another 1.5 hours.

Total Time Expenditure: 8+1+9+1.5+1.5 = 21 hours.

Remaining Time in a Day: 3 hours.

If that goes in a tutorial, WHAT is the essence of YOUR life?

<u>Money:</u>

A typical tutorial charges anywhere between ₹30,000 to ₹1 lakh per year, based on its reputation. Let us consider ₹30,000 including taxes for a single year.

Statistics says that, on an average, a student travels 6−10 kilometres to a tutorial. That is around ₹15−30 in fuel/bus fare per day and approximately ₹800−1000 per month.

Books and miscellaneous costs will go up to ₹3000 per year.

Hence, total expenditure:

30,000+ (800•10) + 3000= ₹41,000 per year.

An average student attends tutorial for 6 academic years before graduation, which sums up to ₹2.5 lakh taking into consideration the calculations above. If this amount is invested suitably; by the time the student gets a job in a few years, he/she will have the fabulous sum of ₹5 lakh in his/her account!

> # If A Student Doesn't Attend Tutorials, He/She Will Turn 'Half A Millionaire' By The Time He/She Gets A Job!

<u>6 Reasons NOT to join a tutorial:</u>

- Joining a tutorial is *not the only option* to score more. There are many other choices.
- Studying and scoring more is just a part of your life. Don't overdo it and torture yourself. Maximize your *efficiency* than the *time* you put in.
- Smart self-study for 1-2 hours a day from the start of the academic year has proved to help 10 times more than a tutorial. Try it. *Doing* is better than just passive *listening*. More on this later.
- Invest the same amount of time in constructive hobbies. This energises and refreshes you; and enables you to concentrate better.
- If you didn't understand something, assertively meet your teacher in person and admit it. Don't allow him/her to go home until the concept is clear. Squeeze the lemon till the last drop. Go to the head of the department if needed. There is no need to join a tutorial to bridge a minute gap.
- As explained earlier, you can save both money and time. Discard the standard flow-chart to *live*!

***

"Ok, show me your bank balance, Mr. Millionaire," I mocked Sridhar.

"Haha, I didn't save, but have invested in lots of good books, and bought myself a decent computer. I am happy with that," he replied, with his head held high. Few mature at a young age like him, which makes creatures like me feel so inferior!

"So what should I do? Quit the tutorial and mug things up from the textbook?" I couldn't make sense of the situation.

"Didn't I tell you about the *Naughty-Note?*" he tore a page and started scribbling.

Naughty-Note is a unique technique which provides you with a crystal clear image of each chapter, helping you reproduce them easily on the exam sheet.

***

Mahesh has two weeks for his test and is in a Catch-22 situation about choosing the study material he can bank upon. He has 4 options to choose from:

1. The Govt. text book which his course has prescribed. He had purchased it paying double the MRP, as the book was out-of-stock.

2. The guide books which his father bought him. Every week-end, his father complains, "I have spent a thousand rupees on the Guide books for your studies. Have you at least turned the pages? When will you progress in life?"

3. The tutorial notes. This has many blank pages on vital topics, due to his bunking.

4. The photocopied notes which his friend has given him. These were the same notes which his senior used to study and pass the exam. The problem is not that it has turned yellow and brittle, or that it has silver fish in it. The problem is that the syllabus has changed!

This question wouldn't have arisen if he had maintained his own notes. <u>*Naughty-Note* technique is nothing but creating your own notes!</u>

Whether you're in a high school, college or in a profession, the ability to take effective and meaningful notes is a crucial skill that is rarely taught.

Note-making is not copying huge chunks of information from books. Notes should act as a trigger to help you recall what you read/heard.

The Purpose of note-taking is simple: To help you study better.

The notes need not contain *everything*, but only *important* artifacts. It must answer **5 *Wives and 1 Husband* – W**hy, **W**hat, **W**here, **W**hen, **W**hom and **H**ow?

Four major reasons for note-making:

1. Even though your writing style resembles that of a doctor's prescription, they are easily understandable and graspable to you as they are in your handwriting.

2. The notes contain already digested concepts pictured sequentially. It is easier to get energised by honey than from *gobi-manchurian*.

3. You will not have any confusion about which material to refer to. Exams will be a cake walk.

4. Studies show that students who take better notes perform better!

3 thumb rules for note-making:

1. **<u>Relevant and accurate:</u>**

   - Focus on points that directly relate to or illustrate your reading and which you are not aware of. Write down key points, theories, definitions, formulae, facts, etc. Make note of diagrams, charts and important examples.
   - Emphasise on the accuracy of the data being recorded.

2. **Keep it simple, silly:**
   - Let notes be brief. It is time-consuming to take down every single word spoken. Use symbols to simplify such as:

What you really mean	Symbol/ Abbreviation
With respect to, that is, which is	Wrt, i.e., viz.
Between, before	b/w, b/4
Divided by, and, not equal	÷ , &, !=
Number, percentage, thousand	#, %, k
Infinite, at, micro, with, without	∞, @, µ, w/, w/o
Example, et cetera, versus	E.g., etc, vs.
Quarter, half, three fourth	¼, ½, ¾
Greater than, lesser than	>, <
Therefore, because	Three dots

   - Circle terms if you don't understand them.
   - Leave spaces or put dotted lines if you fall behind, and ask your teacher to repeat and slow down if required.

3. **Action:**
   - Before Class:
     (a) Glance through the chapter in the text book which is to be taught the next day.

     (b) Recognise the questions bubbling in your mind so you can get them answered the next day.

   - During Class:
     (a) Once you have a bird's eye view of the chapter to be taught, pay attention to the cues during the class and prioritise the information.

     (b) The cues can be: vital statistics, repetitions, word signals (such as, 'first point, second, third'), summaries, dates of events, important names of people, block diagrams, theories, definitions, images, formulae or your own questions.

(c) Often, teachers may say: "Write this down, it's important". Mark these instances with a symbol such as //XXX//.

- After the class:
  (a) Reorganise your notes as needed; create maps, charts and summaries; use various coloured pens to highlight or identify vital information.

  (b) Review the notes the same day, not on the night before an exam; and identify the concepts in which you need further clarification.

  (c) Evaluate the quality of your notes – are you on the right track? Are there errors? How to improve? Ask your teacher to review and make suggestions for your improvement.

Notes should be short, to the point, well organized and an easy read. These three tools help in note making.

Tool 1: Gimme Bullets

Tool 2: Spidey-Map

Tool 3: Cornell System

Tool 1: <u>Gimme bullets</u>

Capturing the hierarchical relationships of data is best done using bullets. They work well when the material has to be well organised, and when the information moves from main ideas to supporting detail.

Most of this book follows this method to ensure you grasp the idea well.

E.g.: Notes on Advantages of <u>LASER</u>, from a high-school lecture.

LASER

- *Light Amplification by Stimulated Emission of Radiation*
- *Types*
  - *1) Ruby LASER*
  - *2) He-Ne LASER*
  - *3) Semi-cond Diode LASER*
- *Advtgs*
  - *<u>Medicine</u>: Bloodless surgery, laser healing, eye and kidney treatments, dentistry, cosmetic*
  - *<u>Industry</u>: Cutting, Welding, marking and heating parts*
  - *<u>Military</u>: Target markings, missile defense, alternatives to RADAR*
  - *<u>Law Enforcement</u>: Finger print and forensic dept.*
  - *<u>Research</u>: LASER annealing, scattering, interferometry, LIDAR, etc.*
  - *<u>Commercial Pr.dev</u>: Printers, Scanners, optical discs, holograms.*
  - *<u>Entertainment</u>: LASER light shows.*

This way of writing notes is better than multiple pages of descriptive explanation.

Tool 2: <u>Spidey-Map</u>

A Spidey-map or *Mind-map* is a visual form of note-taking.

The teacher may jump around the topic, explore a lot of ideas during the lecture, divert due to a question asked by your classmate, wander to a different chapter and then come back to the present topic. Often, a point narrated later in the lecture may relate better to the main topic. This might force us to flip back and forth to find where the information goes best, or risk losing the information just said and what he/she said before. This tool tackles these situations best.

Few argue that the visual format helps more than traditional note-taking; as a well-known saying goes, 'A picture is worth a thousand words'. This also creates a buzz in both left and right sides of the brain due to the creativity involved.

One simple way to understand this is by comparing it to a map of, say, Bangalore city. The city centre (marked as 'Bangalore') represents the main idea; the main roads leading from the centre represent the key information in your thought process.

> A *Spidey-map* converts monotonous information into a colourful, memorable and highly organized diagram which makes the brain ready to suck in the whole idea; retain, brainstorm and summarize.

To *Spidey-map* a lecture, you simply write the main topic of the day's lecture at the centre of the sheet- this is called the *main idea*. As the teacher makes new points, write those around it, which are known as the *branches*. The *branches* may further divide into sub-points called *twigs*. Draw lines connecting different ideas. Render the map with images more than words.

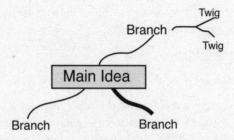

Maps are not restricted to any patterns, but can be formed in a variety of shapes depending upon what you want to illustrate.

The map can even include **flow charts and diagrams**.

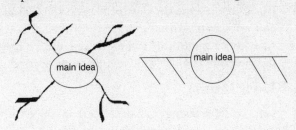

E.g.: Simple map on Photosynthesis

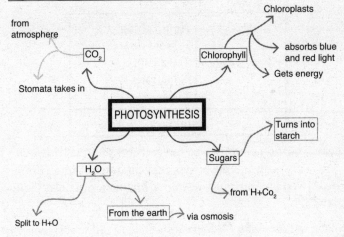

Note:

- Your brain will be more excited by thick curvy lines than straight, monochromatic ones.
- Throw in keywords, play and brainstorm; the number of branches depends on the idea and purpose. Don't leave out anything in creating maps.
- By using only one word per branch, you multiply the number of possibilities in the thought process.
- Attach more paper if necessary. We don't have a 'one-page-only' rule. Symbols can be used to cue the next page.

- Do not be discouraged if some of your branches get stuck. Just resume the flow of ideas at the central idea and work your way out again.
- Apart from notes, this technique can also be used for presentations, problem solving, planning a speech, etc.

Tool 3: <u>Cornell System</u>

This system of note-taking was developed in the 1950's by Professor Walter Pauk of Cornell University. This is one of the most organised ways of preparing notes.

	<u>Note Taking</u>
<u>Key Words</u>	1. Note-down 2. Introspect 3. Narrate 4. Revise
<u>Summary</u>	

Divide your page into two columns. Label the smaller left column 'Keywords' and the bigger right column as 'Note Taking'. These two columns must rest on a foundation named 'Summary'.

Follow the *Nirmal is **IN** Rome* technique to utilise this tool.

N: Note down, I: Introspect, N: Narrate, and R: Revise.

<u>Note down:</u>

(a) During the lecture, write your notes in the 'Notes' column. The motto is to capsulate facts, statistics and the main points of the lecture.

(b) After the lecture, reduce each note into a keyword and enter it in its respective field in the 'Keyword' column.

Introspect:

   (a) Cover the 'Note taking' column with a sheet of paper, but leave the 'Keywords' column visible.

   (b) Introspect using only the 'Keywords' column. By glancingatyourkeywords, trytorecallyournotes. Talk out loud.

   (c) When you're done, uncover the 'Note taking' column to verify what you said or imagined.

Narrate:

   (a) Take a 5 minute break.

   (b) Now narrate the whole topic to yourself/friend. The accuracy of the idea you narrated shows the degree of your comprehension.

   (c) **When you're done doing this exercise, write a brief summary of the notes in the 'Summary' section.**

Revise:

   (a) As the retention of knowledge decreases with time, it is advisable to revise any topic every week.

E.g.: Date: 1/9/2013, Subject: Social Studies, Topic: Jallian-wala Bagh Massacre

Keywords Column	Note Taking column
What happened?	Massacre killing > 1k and injuring 1.5k people incl. women, elderly and kids
Where? When?	Jallianwala Bagh garden during Baisakhi celebration, Amritsar, on 13th Apr 1919
Why? Who killed?	Attack led by Gen. Dyer assuming that 15-20k people met to rebel against British
Sequence: Dyer 1650 rounds	Dyer and 50 riflemen surrounded the garden, fired 1650 rounds for approx.. ten minutes, until the ammunition supply was over. People ran all over, few jumped into well, only to be killed or wounded.
Aftermath: Shook-protests, Knighthood, Dyer pre-planned and killed	• Incident shook the country, and protests mushroomed all over leading to further violence. • Rabindranath Tagore renounced his knighthood as 'a symbolic act of protest' to the Viceroy Lord Chelmsford. • Dyer's action was found to be pre-planned and approved by the British Lt. Governor Michael O' Dwyer, who was later shot and killed by Udham Singh on 13 Mar 1940.

Summary:13th Apr 1919 − a Black day in History − killing/injuring thousands of innocent people − in Jallianwala Bagh-pre-planned by Dwyer − led by Gen. Dyer and other 50 riflemen − incident shook India − protests mushroomed − Dwyer killed by Udham Singh

***

Chapter Seven:

Secret #5: Stand and Deliver

"The best way to make your dreams come true is to wake up."

–Paul Valery

"In the last ten thousand years, many rulers from all over the world have invaded India. Right from the Greeks, Turks, Mughals, Portuguese, French, Dutch to the British. But we Indians have not conquered even a single country and yet, Indian inventions and concepts are found in every corner of the world. Is there any other country with such diversity and tolerance in its political leadership?

Our map structure changed. Naming conventions changed – Mountain Sagar Matha was renamed Mt. Everest, Kalighat became Kolkata, Durjayalinga became Darjeeling, Kodagu became Coorg, Madikeri became Markera, Bhagyanagar turned Hyderabad, and so on. Even our relatives – chacha-chachis, bhayya-bhabhis, all turned into uncles and aunties! Moreover, we had to undergo a lot of changes and compromises to our socio-economic parameters as well.

It has been estimated that the total amount of treasure that the British looted from India by 1901, was equal to 1 billion pounds! Considering interest rates and inflation, it now comes to around a loss of $1 trillion to India. That is, 1 followed by 12 zeros!

Yet, there is no dearth of resources in India.

Many civilizations disappeared. The Greek civilization didn't see another Socrates, Euclid, or Pythagoras. Mesopotamia disappeared; the places are there, but what about the civilisation? The Roman civilisation didn't see another Caesar. Whereas populations increase with time, we have the Mayan population which diminished from 50 million to a mere 60 thousand, in just 500 years! The same trend holds good for Egyptians, the Incas, etc.

But what about our Indian civilization? We have multiplied in number, in strength and potential. Scientists like C.V. Raman, Martyrs like Bhagat Singh, Entrepreneurs like Ratan Tata are still taking birth. We are seeing growth in terms of per capita income, productivity, exports, man power, capability, etc, at a healthy pace.

Don't you think we have the stamina? YES, INDIA HAS THE STAMINA TO SUSTAIN!"

Kumar ended his talk *against* the motion of the debate competition: '*India Doesn't Have the Stamina to Sustain*', and we, the 9th standard who were the audience, stood up with roaring applause, appreciating his views and his data-driven talk. No surprise, it was Kumar who won first place.

A student delivering such a well-thought out talk in a school is rarely expected. The whole day was an autograph session for him. However, that didn't mean that he was not approachable.

He was elected as class leader and he literally behaved as one. The way he would treat people and solve their issues outshone even an airhostess. Plus, he would score decently in exams!

I was happy at the way my close friend was being treated, as he totally deserved it. But what was stopping me from learning his secrets?

When Kumar and I were playing badminton near my home during the summer holidays, my neighbour Preeti had joined us. Preeti is beauty personified, a lass from Delhi, settled in Bangalore, and of our age. And there you go, Kumar was cupid-struck! Though he gave her plenty of signs of being attracted to her, she barely spoke or glanced at him.

I had nothing to gain to stop him, because of 3 reasons:

1. The day my mom introduced her to me, it was the *Rakhi* festival, and I was forced to become her brother. Sometimes traditions play spoilsport.

2. Trying for a girl next door though easy, is *highly risky*. Risk quadruples if your mom is sensitive towards rumours from the neighbourhood.

3. Preeti is fair, Kumar is dark; I have no problem in watching a black and white movie.

As we were playing badminton singles, he tried two ways to gain her attention:

- First, he snatched my racquet from me and started playing with her with full vigour. He purposefully lost in the beginning, praised her; and later started winning skillfully. That didn't work.
- As he had to concentrate more on the shuttlecock, he got less time to stare at her. So, he let me play and resumed what he did best.

Nevertheless, she didn't pay him any attention. A sad story. In addition, Kumar thinks I hadn't noticed what he did, poor boy!

I convinced him about orchestrating a win-win situation: he teaching me his secrets of outshining the class, and I helping him in Preeti's case. It worked!

***

Kumar, many years ago, used to get up each day and feel that:

- Jail was a better place than school. He had no good friends, and the world had turned bland.
- His self-esteem was getting lower by the day, similar to the rupee against the dollar. This was making him less energised to study.
- Life had become like an *Angry-Birds* game. All the attacking birds had unique powers: teachers scold, friends thrash, society vilifies, parents curse.
- There is no respect to be got, even from his dog Rosy.
- Standing on stage was riskier than entering a radioactive region.
- Life sucks, 100 times more than the tentacles of an octopus.

However, one day, when he was walking by a library, he read a quote:

> **There are two rules of life, no matter if you accept them or not:**
>
> <u>Rule A:</u> **This is YOUR life**
>
> <u>Rule B:</u> **Like everybody, even you'll have problems; and two options to deal with them: One: Be upset that you have a problem. Two: Take charge and solve it.**

He chose the second option. He researched on how to get over low self-esteem, talk on stage and make friends.

> **Studies say that as part of your extra-curricular activities, if you are a confident person, an emphatic speaker and if people like you, you not only feel a great deal of empowerment and positive self-esteem but as a side-effect you will be motivated to succeed in the curriculum as well! Two birds with one stone.**

He stumbled upon two tools:

> ## Tool 1: *Stand & Deliver*
> ## Tool 2: 6 *Magnets*

<u>Tool 1:</u> **Stand & Deliver**

This tool will help you in delivering an interesting talk.

Have you had a chance to listen to any speech from a local politician? It is usually pure torture:

- As usual his speech will be in the second half of the function. 95% of the crowd will be waiting for the 'free lunch' planned after the event.
- People are already bored, with both the event and the state of affairs. They will be expecting a dull and repetitive talk.

- The local politician comes on the dais, holds the microphone, blows on it hard to ensure it is working, and starts his speech.
- *"Respectad ghests aan the dayaas namely, tha cheep gheest Babulal-ji, Somulal-ji, Bhabi-ji, respectad cummissionar Raghav-ji, Panchaayat membars Pappu-ji, Gappu-ji, Jija-ji, Saccha-ji, accha-ji; yuuth membars namely Batukes, Rajes, Bhames; paarty membars, cummunitey membars and tha residants aaf our areaa. I wud naat have cumm today becaase aaf anather fankshan in Malapur. Butt, as our Sunaina medam ji rikkested, I cud naatt say NO to har, so here I yam standing in frant aaf you to give speech…"*
- A Catch-22 situation for the crowd, whether to escape this torture or to bear it for the sake of the free lunch.

This is the worst way to deliver a speech. Feel sorry for such a politician, for he may never grow beyond his village.

There are much better ways of giving a speech, believe me!

Any speech may be trifurcated as follows:

- The start: This must contain a hook to grab the attention of the audience, followed by a formal introduction to the speaker and the subject.
- The middle: The essence of the topic has to be revealed here.
- The end: The summary, followed by another hook to make a mark on the listener's mind.

In ancient times, talks by speakers would go on for hours. That was the only source of entertainment and news for people. People were in no hurry to get to the end of the speech because there were no other distractions.

However, today we have nothing but diversions. We live in a different version of the world due to the invention of the television, internet, cell-phones, etc. This asks for a refinement in the way information is presented.

This tool will throw light on:

    1) Attention grabbing

    2) 11 templates to deliver a great speech.

(a) <u>Attention grabbing</u>

> **First, A Speaker Must Grab The Attention Of The People. Only Then Can He Give *Gyaan* Or Convey A Message.**

The rule to grab the attention in a talk is: 'White rat stole a cookie'.

White <u>RAT</u> Stole a Cookie:

- **W- Wit**
- **R- Reveal**
- **A- Ask**
- **T- Tale**
- **S- Statistics**
- **C- Curiosity**

<u>Wit:</u>

Say, Pramod is addressing a State Youth Union meeting. He can start his talk in this fashion:

A thief stops a posh car in an uninhabited area and demands, "Give me all the money you have, or else I'll kill you!" The person was coincidentally a politician and says, "Hey, I am an MLA, how can you steal from me?" The thief laughs out loud and replies, "Then, give me MY MONEY or else I'll kill you!"

Friends, the whole world is aware of the current state of our government. Isn't this high time for us to step up and clean it?

– Pause–

Good morning all, my name is Pramod and I am today's MC for the function.

The whole gathering will be impressed by the opening shot Pramod has hit! Each time he holds the mike, automatically, people will be all ears.

Accomplished speakers often begin their talk with a humorous incident or anecdotes or use some unique witty repartee, which is apt for the event. This hook will gain immediate attention. On the flip side, if the audience fails to grasp the humor, it can be a disastrous start!

Let's assume Gowri is campaigning for the 'College Head' post in a class of 4th Semester students. She can start as follows:

All these days, I have campaigned in front of 5th and 6th semester students in all the divisions. One friend of mine asked me, "Gowri, why haven't you campaigned in the 4th semester yet?" Now, having met so many wonderful and loving people here, I realise what she meant. Let me thank you from the bottom of my heart…

After this start, Gowri establishes a strong 'connect' with the audience.

Using wit to start a talk is a challenge, but if successful, you win the audience's heart.

Reveal:

The easiest way of gaining attention is by holding up some object/exhibit for people to look at. People will be fascinated and will heed anything that is dynamic. This technique can be employed before a dignified audience.

A simple example is of slides being projected on a screen. The below is another example of how a hotel manager from Delhi started his speech:

Ladies and gentlemen, behold, this is the golden pen which Shah Rukh Khan presented me when I was in Mumbai. Not because I am special, not because he had too many pens to give away. But out of liking for the hospitality I showered on him at the hotel in spite of the monsoon floods.

Ask:

Filling a void with interaction or by questioning or throwing a challenge to the audience is a very powerful way of opening a talk.

The use of this opening makes the audience synchronise with the speaker. This is the best technique for beginners and can be tested when other methods feel ineffective.

George initiated his biology seminar in this approach:

Name a few enzymes present in our body. Let us see how many friends seated here are intelligent!

Be sure with the correctness of your answer. If your reply is erroneous, you'll turn into a laughing stock!

Tale:

Why does cinema attract people? Because everybody likes stories!

A relevant story, if managed well can turn out to be a grand opening for a talk. Such a start can hardly fail and hence, is a good bet for beginners.

Example:
Long ago, there was a young wood cutter. Each day he carried his sharp axe to the forest, to chop wood. On the first day, he was able to fell 10 huge trees. On the second day, he felled 8 huge trees; the third day 5 trees. Though his energy level and working hours were the same, the end result was getting worse with time. By the end of the sixth day, he was able to fell only a single tree. What was the reason?

– Pause –

He didn't sharpen his axe! He was working harder, but not sharper. Friends, don't you think we are doing the same thing? We need to scale up in order to get the expected results.

With such a start, the speaker will dominate the gathering during the entire talk.

Statistics:

Have you observed the traffic in this city? The delay due to traffic has increased by 35% in a mere 3 years! The accident numbers have doubled in the last five years. Friends, looking at this trend, it is time for us, the Automobile Engineers, to invent an alternate means of transportation to ease such commuting woes.

If this is a sensible start by a speaker in an engineers' club, the crowd gets motivated, plus, never gets diverted from the speech.

The advantage of this type of start is:

- You can sometimes use 'made-up' statistics. But be as close to the real figure as far as possible.
- 98.9% of folks will never realise that it was a false number (including this statistic), plus, they feel that you've researched to get the data because you are more intelligent than them!

Curiosity:

The next ten minutes could change your life.

People like talks that piqué their curiosity; and this is undoubtedly the best technique to start your talk.

Long ago, in a dark, dark wood, there lived a horrible horrendous, terrible tremendous… human-like entity, which everybody had declared dead fifteen years ago. What he was up to that summer night was terrifying…

The crowd will start wondering what you are going to say and will hold on to their chairs with suspense!

Another technique of gaining attention is by maintaining absolute silence for about a minute. The audience will wonder whether you have forgotten your script!

(b) 11 Templates To Deliver A Brilliant Speech:

1. What people see is what they believe. You will be judged by the way you arrive on stage. Appear bright, smart and confident before them. Giving a talk is no less than selling yourself!

2. Use your natural voice and accent to talk. If you pretend to be a *Pardesi Babu* and try to impress, people will realise it!

3. Use power words: *"Yes, we can succeed!"* Don't beat around the bush. A person's attention will not last more than 15 minutes.

4. You must *wait*. Absolutely! You must pause:

    (a) When somebody is talking in the group. Stop and stare at them. They'll shut up when they realise that they are being observed.

    (b) When the audience is laughing, so that they settle down!

    (c) After asking a stimulating question.

5. Prepare. Prepare and prepare. It takes a minimum of 2 hours to prepare for a perfect one minute talk! And never memorise the talk.

6. Get rid of 75% of your nervousness. The remaining 25% is required for you to be mentally alert on stage!

7. Which is the most precious asset a person can have? Enthusiasm. Never lessen it on stage.

8. If Rahul is holding the mike and says something like, "I will tell you a joke," or, "I am not prepared to talk today," or, "What can I say when the earlier learned speakers have spo-

ken so well," and so on, he'll become a jerk for the people. Instead, say whatever comes to mind, like how we talk to our friends. Just say what you ought to, and then sit down!

9. Take questions at the end. If people talk in-between, you'll lose the momentum.

10. Your tone will deliver 80% of the message. The words you speak account for just 20% unless you are the Prime Minister.

11. Start and end like a champion. Exploit the 'White RAT Stole a Cookie' rule to the fullest.

<u>Tool 2:</u> 6 Magnets

Long ago, there was a young man in America who was not doing well as a salesman. As his life was not going the way he wanted it to, people say that he had decided to commit suicide. Meanwhile, he got a brilliant idea! 'Why can't I find out why so many people are successful?' He took a pen and pad, and began interviewing the most successful people in town.

After 6 years of research, when the young man compared the notes, he stumbled upon some common traits. He compiled them, and printed a book containing all those principles.

Over a million copies were sold in a short span! The title of the book was, 'How To Win Friends And Influence People' and the author was – Dale Carnegie.

The below 6 magnets are based on the principles he found.

<u>Magnet 1:</u>

Don't Criticise, Condemn or Complain

A study says that, when murderers, thieves, dacoits are interviewed in jails, they defend themselves saying, they are not the culprits; and start explaining how the judges and lawyers were wrong, or the way the police mismanaged the case and so on.

If a murderer is not ready to accept his mistake and take the criticism, will a dignified person bear such criticism?

If you condemn, the other person will only distance himself from you. This is a hard truth. "Any fool can condemn, criticize or complain; and most fools do," a saying goes.

Follow this, and instantaneously people will start liking you.

Magnet 2:
Give Honest and Sincere Appreciation

If you go to your knowledgeable neighbour who is fat, and say, "Nikhil, today you are looking very slim. Have a great day!" Then, it is flattery.

On the other hand, if you tell him, "Nikhil, yesterday, my brother and I were talking about the amazing knowledge you have. We are glad to have a neighbour like you. Have a great day!" This is honest appreciation.

Flattery comes from the lips; honest and sincere appreciation comes from the heart. Note that, even in failures or heartbreak you can find a constructive aspect.

Initially when you appreciate somebody, you may feel discomfort; through practice you will become an expert and this will make you popular!

Magnet 3:
Arouse In the Other Person An Eager Want

Sumanth is a manager in a private firm. He wanted hard copies of 20 pages typed and edited on a priority basis. However, the office typist Suma was occupied in other activities. If Sumanth goes to her abruptly and orders her to do the job for him, she might make excuses and postpone it, or do an error-ridden job.

As Sumanth is a smart manager, he goes to her and says, "Hi Suma, you have been doing great work these days, when can I see you as a senior typist?" Suma is on cloud nine, as nobody in the office has ever spoken to her in this manner. "Hello sir! Thanks for your positive comments. I will do my best to scale up," she replies.

This is the time Sumanth should try to capitalise upon the already set stage. "That's great, Suma. For a sincere and hard-working person like you, it should not take more than half an hour to type these 20 pages, right?" Suma invariably agrees to Sumanth and does the job in just 25 minutes, plus, she double checks for any spelling errors and then submits them.

If the other person has an eager want, he/she will do the job with utmost care and involvement. Exploit this to get things done, plus the bonus of an improved relationship.

Magnet 4:

Become Genuinely Interested In the Other Person, Listen to Him, And Talk on His Terms

There is a doctor named Sughosh Mehra in my neighborhood. Due to his correct analysis of both the patient and the symptom, he is able to cure his patients with great efficiency. The problem is, he is not ready to expand his small clinic and due to the high inflow of patients, the clinic resembles a local train in peak hours!

Last year on July 1st, I was suffering from viral fever and visited his clinic. As usual, it was a fish market and I was the 27th person in queue. According to my calculations, it would take at least 3 hours for my turn to arrive. How to pass the time? Coughing and shivering are the usual options when you are unwell. Luckily, I was able to snatch a single sheet of the Times of India newspaper from the 26th person in the queue. I had all the time in the world to mug it up, give a lecture to the surrounding people and eventually get some thundering applause.

The headline read as follows: 'National Doctor's Day to be celebrated today'.

Right away I escaped from the queue, bought a rose from the neighboring florist, came back to the clinic and convinced the receptionist that I have no ailment and just wanted to wish the doctor. Like an angel, she heeded my request, and I was the next person in!

"Doctor Mehra, I wish you a very happy national doctor's day!" I said him, and presented the red rose I had bought for ₹5. He was delighted, "Thanks a lot! I am glad somebody remembers it. I definitely needed this, please sit down, may I know your name?"

"Doctor, I am Chandan, your old patient. Let's talk about me later. Tell me doctor; you cure the ailments of so many patients with a staggering rate of efficiency! How do you manage to do it? By the way, how is *your* health? Are you having food on time or have you lost your appetite in serving people? You have become so much thinner than the last time I saw you."

He was so pleased! He began explaining how he did his MBBS in spite of his poor financial background, about his marriage to a gynaecologist, his health, etc. His speech ran for about 15 minutes, but I was all ears.

Involuntarily, I coughed and sneezed, one after the other. The doctor got worked-up, "Chandan, you didn't tell me that you have a cold? Come let me test you!"

He brought his stethoscope near my chest, analyzed my symptoms, and scribbled something on the prescription. He also called the receptionist inside and said, "From now on, if this young man comes to our clinic, let him in without an appointment. And waive today's consultation fees".

"Thank you again for coming by, get well soon!" he continued and winked at me.

In the 21st century, did a mere ₹5 help me break a queue of 26 people, make the doctor concerned about my simple viral fever, waive the consultation fee, and get me a priority entry for future appointments for free? Yes it did!

Become genuinely interested in the other person; let him do the talking on his terms. You simply have to listen. Eventually, people will fall in love with you!

<u>Magnet 5:</u>

Smile

Most of us have only two buttons in our remote:

- Button 1: Look serious like a dumb boss.
- Button 2: Laugh out loud like a mad person.

We seem to miss-out on the 3rd button – a SMILE!

Even in hilarious standup comedy shows, a few people sitting in the front row will never laugh, they even curb their smiles. They are afraid that their social prestige is at stake, they suffer from *What-if-somebody-sees-me-smiling* syndrome. These are the people who die early!

Once, in a hurry, Ritwik jumped a signal in a busy main road and unfortunately a traffic policeman caught him red-handed. To add to his woes, he wasn't even carrying his driving license and RC book!

Ritwik removed his helmet, smiled generously at the policeman and apologised for his mistake. The policeman, asked for his DL and RC book. Even this didn't stop Ritwik from smiling. The policeman looked at him from top to bottom. The person, who usually made a few quick bucks in such cases, let him go and said, "Go! Run from here. You look like a decent young man. I am letting you go only because of your smiling face; never repeat such a mistake."

This simple five letter word simply attracts people!

Magnet 6:

A Man's Name to Him Is the Sweetest Sound in Any Language.

When a newly married couple shows their wedding photos to you, what do we do?

- Our eyes stealthily searches for ourselves in the photo.
- The photographs in which we are not present appear dry and lifeless, and we don't think twice about turning the pages of the album.

- If you are present in a particular photo, a bright aura reflects on your face and you look at it from all angles, comment, show it to others and rejoice!

For a man, he, himself, is the most important person in the world.

Similarly, his name is the sweetest sound in any language. We often take the people who do less skilled work, for granted. For example, we say, "Hey driver, go bring the car". Instead, if we say, "Hey Ramu, please bring the car", his self-esteem will be boosted and he will work with an extra pinch of zeal.

***

"Wow Kumar, what great insights! Instead of thanking you let me grant you a boon – *Sheegrameva* Preeti *Praptirastu*," I giggled at Kumar.

He came to my home that evening. Agenda: to meet Preeti.

Unusually, her home was in the process of being packed-up

swiftly; a huge van was being dumped with all the goods. I called her out to enquire.

"Hi Chandan, Hi Kumar," she said and came out. Kumar's shirt collar rose, as she had called his name. "My father has been transferred to Gujarat and we are also moving out with him. All this happened in a hurry," she said in her familiar sweet tones. Her dimple was a treat to watch.

This is the major side effect of a central govt. job: transfers. And as a result, my friend Kumar had to pay the fine as well!

Kumar opened his somber mouth, "I am sad you are moving out, Preeti… err…. Let me help you in packing things up."

"Thanks a lot, Kumar. The packers and movers are doing it all and we are almost through. I will let you know my local contact number when I reach Gujarat. I will surely miss you all!" she said and we parted ways.

The huge van was playing a sad song, most suitable to Kumar's condition.

***

Chapter Eight:

Secret #6: Time Machine

"Don't be fooled by the calendar. There are only as many days in the year as you make use of. One man gets only a week's value out of a year while another man gets a full year's value out of a week."

— Charles Richards

Thursday was the most awaited day in school. The reason – sports period for 3 hours!

The school playground would be divided into 3 sub-play-grounds: one for cricket, one for football and the remaining for throw-ball. Girls had one third reservation, so we boys gave away the lazy throw-ball section. Though the ground was trifurcated, it didn't stop the players and balls from moving back and forth throughout the field.

Football was the preferred game for 30% of the boys in the class, including myself and Ashish. The remaining guys chose cricket though most of them would spend time only fielding.

Ashish was from Gujarat, and the all-rounder of the class. He was good at studies, attended theatre classes in the evening, aerobic classes in the early morning and yet seemed to have ample relaxation time. He had mastered time.

Coincidentally, he was a neighbour and the envy of boys my age. In Science, there is something called *theoretical value* and *practical value*. Experiments are usually judged by comparing both. Ashish was the *theoretical value*.

Our parents had a common answer to all our questions:

- Question: I will be late today, special classes; fine?

  Answer: *Ashish will also be with you, right?*

- Q: Pa, can I go to a trek?

  A: *Go only if Ashish is going.*

- Q: Can I have a computer?

  A: *See, Ashish is managing without it. Learn from him.*

- Q: I'm not in the mood to study. Can I sleep for a while?

  A: *Look at Ashish. Will he also be sleeping? When will you learn?*

Coming back to the sports period, in football, I was often made the goal keeper as I was chubby. And due to repeated practice, I had become proficient in saving goals. Ashish on the other hand was a skillful *forward*. We both, though good friends were mostly put in different teams, and would turn into cut-throat rivals on the football field.

The game kicked off and the excitement started right away. Ashish swiftly cut through our team's *mid-fielders* as well as the *defenders* in no time. Within a few seconds, it was me versus Ashish. He had all the time in the world to score. He was readying his right leg to kick and score a goal, and put his rival team under pressure right away. *He was kicking from his right leg from his right side, which at the present angle would make the ball approach me to my right.* Assessing his move, very smartly, I attacked him and defended the goal fruitfully!

His expression held a tinge of both anguish and surprise, whereas my team was happy with my brave efforts.

Time flew and we had scored 1 goal whereas Ashish's team had scored nil.

It was half-time.

Ashish came to me and whispered, " Chandu, we are friends right, then allow me to score a goal next time and level the game 1-1. I'll buy you a cola this evening." He laughed as if he was kidding, but his eyes told a different story.

Three thoughts in my mind:

1. Wow! He thinks I am a good goal keeper! Ok relax, don't be excited.

2. He is desperate to soothe his ego and self-respect, by levelling the score. Act smart.

3. He is trying to bribe a 'bribe-master' who has learnt how to study only by bribing his friends, silly boy!

I told him, "Thanks for the proposal, but I have a better deal. I'll surely allow you to score a goal. In return, you tell me how you manage your time better than anybody else. If you scratch my back, I will scratch yours! Simple." I said. "Plus," I continued, "I will buy *you* a cola this evening!"

The *Gujju* guy was thinking. The break was done; he nodded and smiled in acceptance.

Later, Ashish got energised from nowhere, and scored a goal without my participation! I mean, he just overwhelmed all our players and sliced through my strong defence as well! He winked at me, thinking that I had deliberately allowed him to score a goal. I read his mind, and laughed at his foolishness. The game was tied 1-1. And he kept his word, sincere chap!

***

"Not managing time is like shooting in the dark" – a French proverb.

Shravan is a normal college student whose nickname is 'No-time boy'. The name was derived from a habit of his. If anybody invites him:

- For combined studies, he would say: "I have no time."
- To play? "No time."
- Go hang out? "No time."
- Go to college? "No time."
- Why didn't you score well? "I have no time to study."
- Why are you so fat? "No time to exercise."
- Why have you Blah Blah? "Blah Blah because I have no time."

Like amnesia, cholera and anemia, many have the 'no-timeria' disease. If you examine a school/college, you will find at least 30% of the students have this disease.

Yes, we have two injections to cure this disease:

> # Injection 1: Priority Matrix
> # Injection 2: Weekly Planner

Injection 1: Priority Matrix

Bhargav has two things to do. One, connect his mobile to the charger, two, switch off a leaking gas cylinder. Will he consider the two tasks as having the same priority? What happens if he gives option one the first priority? A disaster!

It has become a common practice for us to blindly do something without putting it in the context of priority first.

The Priority Matrix, (also called the Eisenhower method or ABC analysis) will help you in solving this, by categorising the tasks of the day into 4 well defined priorities:

- Important and Urgent
- Important, but not urgent
- Not important, but urgent
- Not important and not urgent

	Urgent	Not-Urgent
Important	Quadrant 1 Total time here:_____	Quadrant 2 Total time here:_____
Not Important	Quadrant 3 Total time here:_____	Quadrant 4 Total time here:_____

Method of following this:

    (a) All the tasks of the day must be listed on a sheet.

    (b) Each of the tasks must be placed in the corresponding quadrant in the Priority Matrix.

    (c) Estimate the time required to complete each quadrant.

    (d) Post categorisation, we must deal with the tasks according to the quadrant they belong to.

Quadrant 1: This is the sweet spot in which you handle the critical tasks for the day. If a task falls in this quadrant, it conveys that the corresponding task is both important and urgent. *E.g.: Preparing for tomorrow's statistics unit test.*

Quadrant 2: These are the tasks which are important and have to be done, but not immediately. *E.g.: spending 2 hours on a project due one month from now.*

Quadrant 3: Your friend has invited you for a movie which starts one hour from now. This is urgent, but not important. Such tasks must fall under this category.

Quadrant 4: Downloading a torrent file, window shopping in a mall, and other miscellaneous activities which are neither important nor urgent must sit here.

This tool has proved to be a boon for people of all professions and types. You can even download a priority matrix app on your PC or phone for maximum adherence.

Injection 2: Weekly Planner

Sunil could change his D-grades into B grades in his tests, only by using this tool. This, if used diligently, can change your life positively.

This tool is a bird's eye view of how and where you will spend your week.

The tool has 11 columns: Subject, Task number, Tasks, Time, and one column for each day of the week.

Subject	Task no.	Tasks	Weekday	Mon	Tue	Wed	Thu	Fri	Sat	Sun
	1		Time							
	2		5 am							
	3		6 am							
	4		7 am							
	5		8 am							
	6		9 am							
	7		10 am							
	8		11 am							
	9		12 noon							
	10		1 pm							
	11		2 pm							
	12		3 pm							
	13		4 pm							
	14		5 pm							
	15		6 pm							
	16		7 pm							
	17		8 pm							
	18		9 pm							
	19		10 pm							
	20		11 pm							
	21		12 midnight							

A filled template of a 12th standard student, Diana is given below. This is not a one-time-event and the data in the template will change each week.

Subject must contain the subjects which you will study in this week, e.g.: Math, Physics, etc. The roles which you play as a student, a friend, a son, etc. can also come under this parameter.

Jot down the *Tasks* you plan to accomplish against the corresponding *Subject*. Number them using the *Task no.* column.

Subject	Task no.	Tasks	Week day	Mon	Tue	Wed	Thu	Fri	Sat	Sun
Physics	1	Laws of Motion	Time							
	2	Dynamics	5am							
	3	Magnetism	6am	18	18	18	18	18	18	18
Chem-istry	4	Electrolytes	7am							
	5	Stoichiometry	8am							
	6	Chemical Equilibrium	9am							
Math	7	Exponential Functions	10am							
	8	Laws of logarithms	11am							
	9	Trigonometric Graphs	Noon			College			College	
Elec-tronics	10	Diode theory	1pm							
	11	AEC	2pm							
	12	Linear devices	3pm							
English	13	Rightful inheritors	4pm						8	
	14		5pm							
	15		6pm			17				
Misc	16	B'day gift for Rahul	7pm	1					9	
	17	Music class	8pm	5	19	1		3	20	
	18	Aerobics	9pm		12	16	5	7	10	
As a Son	19	Clean my room	10pm		13	4	2			
	20	Bring grocery	11pm	11		6				
	21		12am							

***

Chapter Nine:

10 Step-By-Step Approaches To Be The Star Of The Class This Year

"It's kind of fun to do the impossible"

— Walt Disney

Disclaimer: *Please proceed ONLY if you are serious about becoming the topper of your class. It requires immense self-discipline; and truthfully, not all students can do this. However, if you follow these steps, your triumph is certain.*

"Why are you watching the cricket match now? Those 11 guys will not help you in tomorrow's exam!"

If these words seem familiar and true, think again. Here are the 10 steps to learn from the most patriotic word we Indians could ever imagine – *Cricket*; and be the star of your class this year!

Step 1:

> ## Start your innings with an average of 4-5 runs per over with a target of 300 in 50 overs.

Myth: "I will start studying a week before the exam. I am the hero of last-minute-preparations."

Let us assume that the Indian cricket team has a target of 300 runs in 50 overs against the Australian team. If the captain sends Rahul Dravid and Lakshman (both the best test match players) to open the innings and they score a team total of less than hundred runs in 35 over; what will happen?

1. *The captain gets badly cursed by all the viewers and his credibility will be at stake.*

2. *The next set of batsmen will have to score a minimum run rate of 14 runs for the next 15 overs to win! Their chances of success are debatable.*

If an athlete wants to win an Olympic medal, a study says that he/she starts preparing 2 years prior to the race, winning smaller targets at a time.

You can't get slim or stay fit by working out at a single session; as the saying goes, *'Rome was not built in a day'.*

Follow the below regime to chase a big target:

✓ **Know your destination:** *Dear Auto driver, take me somewhere... err... anywhere.* Do you say this? When we keep track of where we want to go on a weekend, we must also trace the track we want to travel on in life. Follow the first secret to recognise your path.

"If you hit every time, the target is too near or too big." –Tom Hirshfield

✓ **Study for 2-3 hours from the first day of your academic year.** *If you start at 4-5 runs per over for the first 35 overs, you can easily shift into higher gear later to reach a score of 300 plus in a 50 over match.*

Similarly, study for 2-3 hours per day from the first day of the academic year. Math must consume thirty to forty five minutes. Other subjects have to be studied for two hours.

✓ **2-chair technique.** As explained in the Second Secret, this must be followed for 15 minutes to wrap up each study session.

✓ **Read and write constantly.** *Suhas used to exercise in the morning for one hour. He stopped practice for 2 days. He then went into a comfort zone and never resumed his exercise on any day! Therefore, persist and be consistent everyday.*

Practice if broken, is tough to restart. Choose anything, but read something every day.

Follow the steps given in the 2nd chapter before studying. Repeat the steps.

Step 2:

> **Each ball is a potential sixer. Furthermore, know whom you are batting against, so you can take a single on the last ball of the over.**

Myth: "My father says that I need to study at 5 am everyday to score better."

There is no day in which Abbas has not fought with his father about the right 'time' to study. His father stresses early morning study but our hero feels he studies better at night.

There are strange theories explaining various time-slots for better studying; but all these are myths.

The reality is, **the clock has nothing to do with your studying**. If you have an exam at 3pm, you will grasp concepts like a champion at 2:30pm. This proves that it is your energy levels and your intent which determines the end product. Every second, every minute and every hour is the best time to seek knowledge, and comprehend and retain information.

✓ **Injection 1:** If you've got a lot on your mind, before starting, take a moment to clearly plan out what you want to study and the theme for the day. Use the *Injection 1 – Priority Matrix* explained in the 6th secret to simplify this step.

✓ **Three is a crowd**: Combined study has proved to help catalyse conception, analysis, brainstorming and understanding. However, if your study group has three or more numbers, it may turn out to be more of a *movie-critic* team, and it will develop into a *gossip session*. You must be assertive enough to bring back the conversation to the curriculum. Start studying alone or with a small smart group.

✓ **Tell your friends that your study time is sacred.** Follow the *Right click-Reload* tool explained in the second secret. Let your study time be as sharp as a butcher's knife, and free from distractions.

✓ **Location and Posture.** Follow the *Yogananda, Sparkle-shine* and *Radar-Range* tools from the second secret.

✓ **Multiplex theatre:** A multiplex theatre makes you personally feel the story being depicted on screen. How to ensure you have a similar ambience in your study room? Follow the *Peacock* tool from the second secret.

Step 3:

> # Strategic time-outs and drink breaks are compulsory.

<u>Myth</u>: "Let me study for 3 hours continuously without a break."

Studying is like jogging. During the first few minutes of jogging, your zeal is at the peak. With time, you get tired and feel the lack of stamina. If you continue to jog, the speed and distance travelled will be the bare minimum. It is advisable to rest for a while and resume later.

✓ **50-10:** Our concentration and alertness lessen after 50 minutes of involved effort. It has been proved that taking 10 minutes of break for every 50 minutes of study doubles productivity, compared to studying for 3 hours 'at a stretch'.

✓ **Not 10-50! :** 50 minutes of studying must be followed by 10 minutes of break. (*If I get phone calls that you are studying for 10 minutes and resting for 50 minutes, and not scoring marks, I am not responsible.*)

✓ **Civilised Breaks:** These are as important as focussing on studies. These could be a short walk around your home or a brief chat with your family, a short game of carrom, cuddling your dog, gardening, etc.

✓ **It is definitely not** going to play cricket in a field 2 miles away, or watching a movie, or sightseeing near the girl'shostel!

✓ **Mixed farming:** Agricultural land is utilised to grow various greens throughout the year. Similarly, we must not study a single subject throughout the day. Study multiple subjects separated by breaks.

Step 4:

> ### Even Sachin Tendulkar needed a coach.

Myth: "I will be looked upon as a dumbo if I ask for help or question frequently."

This is the usual thought process of a middle-class student, and let me tell you, you are in serious trouble. Asking for help is smart, not stupid.

✓ **Talk to the teachers early:** A study says that 80% of students ask questions or try to get doubts clarified only on the day of the exam! It's too late by then. However, if you want to top the class, talk to the professor often, build rapport; and once you see water seeping into your ship, immediately talk to the Captain!

✓ **Accept that you don't know:** *Sandeep pretended that he knew everything. All the teachers were happy about his frequent 'nodding' of the head. His test results proved otherwise!*

If you have not comprehended something, admit it immediately, bridge the gap and move on. Small cracks can prove costly later!

✓ **Look at educational institutions as an investment:** If you pay, you get something back, as straight as a client-vendor relationship. Ask questions boldly. This point should only encourage you to ask questions about the curriculum and NOT about the credibility of the teacher, mind you!

✓ **I-don't-care:** Teachers would have spent years preparing, researching and qualifying to teach. They can easily sort out the 'no-show' students! And guess what, they don't much care about such guys either!

On the contrary, if you are concerned, dedicated, turning in all the assignments and ready to learn, the teachers will go an extra mile in helping such students out.

Let it be a silly or basic question, do not ask questions for time pass, but to get it clarified.

✓ **Teachers = aliens? :** It may seem ridiculous but so many students feel that teachers do not belong to this world! Please realize that they are humans just like you, they have families, likes, good and bad days, live in a house and lose their loved ones as well. They have their own pressures in life. However, if you find your teacher annoying and their teaching style unsuitable, get your doubts clarified from some other teacher of the same department. However, be diplomatic and ensure nobody is hurt.

<u>Step 5:</u>

Cricketers must attend every practice session.

<u>Myth:</u> "Let me bunk. This is THE worst class I will ever attend; I would rather go watch a movie."

Bunking isn't bad; but bunking often isn't good either!

✓ **Attendance**: *A famous movie director had a vision of making a brilliant movie on a drunkard. In order to feel the situation, make the scenes more realistic, and pen punchy dialogues, he stayed in a bar 24/7 for 4 long months!*

   Showing up is 90% of life. The attendance in the class is conductive to a positive thought process. A study shows that 95% of the toppers had attendance of more than 90%!

✓ **You joined ONLY because of you:** Absolutely! You didn't join this school/college because of somebody else. You keep your results and you keep the certificates, and hence, it is YOU who is responsible to make the most of it and maximise the outcome.

<u>**Step 6:**</u>

Appetite is as important as practice.

<u>Myth</u>: "Mom feeds me delicious Lassi while I study, I will be more healthy. Awesome."

Sumanth ate sumptuous food at home during study holidays. He had to visit the restroom as often during the exam as he visited the kitchen during the holidays.

✓ **Right fuel:** What happens if you fill diesel in your petrol car? A blunder. Similarly, don't munch junk food if your exams are less than a week away. Chomp on home food and let it be light. Overeating makes your brain lazy and sluggish. Fats like oil, cream, butter, ghee and vanaspati will clog the blood vessels that carry blood to the brain – this will make you feel drowsy.

Note: Let your stomach be filled half with food, quarter water and the remaining quarter with air. Rather than having a complete meal twice or thrice a day, eat moderate portions spaced out over four to six small meals a day.

✓ **Study foods:** A study says that Vitamin C, Vitamin B1, B6, B12, Iron, Iodine, etc. are vital ingredients for brain building, memory and decent health. Let your diet include cereals like rice bran, wheat, etc.; vegetables like turnip, ladies finger, bitter gourd, leafy vegetables; lots of pulses; fruits like papaya, strawberry, melons, dry fruits, apricot, apples, nuts, fish and milk products in controlled amounts, etc.

✓ **Snack smart while you study:** Don't wait till you get hungry and then run hunting for eatables. Avoid any snacks or colas which give you a rush of energy, because, after every rush there is a crash, in which the information you studied is lost to an intense desire to sleep. Focus on 'slow release' foods which in turn provide sustained glucose to the brain.

<u>Step 7:</u>

> # You will be on the bench if you have a bad attitude.

<u>Myth:</u> "I am a rich guy, I will attend a tutorial. Marks will come automatically."

Venkat used to say this each time to Vijay. Later the results said a different story: Though both had similar IQs, Venkat who attended tutorials scored less marks than Vijay who didn't attend any extra classes.

✓ Manish, hailing from a village, wanted to study engineering. He came from a vernacular medium school, barely knew English, lacked communication skills; but was rich in dedication and hard work. After 4 years of intense smart work, he became an engineer and got placed in Infosys!

Attitude, not ability, will determine your success in studies and life.

Study a Subject and the Teacher: Mr. Ramanamurthy was a Math teacher in a govt. pre-university college. He was more complicated than his name suggests. As he was not strict and was a dwarf, the whole class used to take him for granted, make fun of him, enjoy, chit-chat and later disperse. A student named Praveen studied the teacher and keenly observed his unique way of solving problems. His good rapport with the teacher enabled proper knowledge flow, and he eventually scored 100 out of 100 in the final Math exam.

People and their outlooks are unique, their way of handling things are equally distinct. **Respect it and deal with it.**

✓ **6 reasons not to attend the tutorials:** Read them, they are explained in the 4th secret.

✓ **We are taught to be afraid:** People enroll for a *life insurance policy* amounting up to 40-50% of their salary! They spend 20 thousand rupees to buy *Reverse Osmosis filter systems*, though their tap water is tested to be soft and pure! *Why are you saying this? What to do?* Go back to the 4th secret.

✓ **Time and money:** Find out how much time and money you save by not attending a tutorial! Refer to the 4th secret.

Step 8:

> ### *Boundaries* Keep The Scoreboard Ticking More Than The Usual *Singles* And *Doubles*.

Myth: "I mug up notes. That's the best way to learn."

This dialogue made sense in the 1970s. Upgrade your ammunition; this is the age of innovation and creativity. Toss out hard work and welcome smart work.

✓ **Entire curriculum memorised:** Studying the text book as-it-is is a thing of the past. We have tools to study in style, remember with ease and deliver at will! Go back to the 3rd secret to revise the tools: **Bedtime stories, let us have a peg, rubber band, and go home.**

✓ **Very-very-Naughty:** You could study in a rock show! If you want to realise the naughty ways of learning, you have come to the right spot. Go learn these 3 tools of writing and rewriting the notes from the fourth secret: **Gimme bullets, Spidey-Map, and Cornell system.**

✓ **Syllabus book under pillow:** *Big electronic outlets don't home-deliver appliances below ₹5 thousand. They focus only on the costlier fast-moving goods.* Similarly, learn the most important facts first. Prepare for the exam based on the weightage of the marks. Syllabus books will help you in zeroing-on the better chapters to study.

Step 9:

> **Even top batsmen suffer from being *out-of-form*, but they can make a *come-back* with a century!**

Myth: "I failed in this exam, I am a loser, let me quit and join the army."

Einstein failed in Math! Sachin was dismissed for zero in his debut match. Yes, s**t happens.

✓ **Dude, you're almost there:** *I agree you have put in your best, you're attending classes, doing the assignments, studying hard and yet the results are not meeting your expectations. You know what? You are not alone. Right now as you read this, there are people waiting outside the operation theatre spending lakhs of rupees and doing their best to get their loved ones to be well; millions are toiling to ensure a square meal for their kids, and so on.*

So here is a piece of advice: Hang in there, and follow the other tips written in this book. If you do so with a right attitude, you are bound to overcome any challenge.

✓ **Turn into an advertiser:** Advertisers tell the customers about how a product/service will help them. Wear his hat, and find the benefits you will get after completing the course with flying colors. This should help.

✓ **Become a counselling expert for a minute:** We Indians are awesome at giving advice! Pretend that you are counseling a teenager about his negative attitude. What advice would you give him?

✓ **This really is fun:** When you conquer this course successfully, you will sit back on your couch someday and laugh about how you thought of quitting the course!

✓ **Don't assume!:** We assume a lot of things, like, **"What am I getting into, I am failing!"**, "I will never succeed", and so on. Go to your teacher and ask him/her. He/she might even say that you are getting better with time!

Step 10:

Players work hard and party harder!

Myth: "I am not supposed to attend any functions or participate in co-curricular activities; this year is a turning point for me."

If anybody says – "You are a student, you only need to study", then, laugh out loud.

✓ **Injection 2:** Read the 6th secret on how to make best use of time using injection 2 – the Weekly Planner.

✓ **Not always:** Studying all the time doesn't work. You will only be overloading yourself with loads of information and stressing out without gain. Zero-in on the time you will study, and enjoy the remaining time!

✓ **Wear other hats:** Not only a student, you play the role of a son/daughter, grandson/granddaughter, friend, brother/sister, cousin, etc. Play quick games like word-building, chess, etc. with them. Enjoy wearing all the hats!

***

Chapter Ten:

Brownie Points

"Too many of us are not living our dreams because we are living our fears."

– Les Brown

If you have come this far, you are serious about improving your life. I sincerely appreciate the efforts you are putting in, and let me congratulate you on your decision!

This calls for some brownie points:

> **As-If technique:** *Ateeth finds Math a tough nut to crack. Whenever he holds the Math text book, he tends to postpone the study time or change the subject itself!*

▶ 'As-If' is the best tool to tackle such scenarios.

- For the next one hour, Ateeth has to behave as if Math is his favourite subject to study. This will make him interested and motivate him to study.

- TV: Each time you wish to pass time watching television, ask yourself a simple question – on which side of the screen do you wish to be?

- You are a genius: Yes, you heard it right. Your brain has trillions of brain cells, billions of neurons. Studies say that we only utilize 2-10% of our brain's capability.

- "The only place where your dream becomes impossible is in your own thinking." - Robert Schuller

▶ **Water water everywhere:** Note that being well-hydrated is essential for optimum brain function. Keep a water bottle handy. Make sure you are not thirsty while studying.

What works and what doesn't:

- Works: Studying to learn; to make learning fun, inspiring and interesting; learning with a plan; perseverance and skill.

- Doesn't work: Studying for the sake of studying; or for marks; fear, others' sake; dull and routine learning; blindly follow and memorising; giving up.

▶ **Use the *Soviet Queen had 4 Rabbits* technique:**

- **S**urvey (S) the text material

- **Q**uestion (Q) the topic

- **R**ead (1st R) actively and search for answers on the topic

- w**R**ite(2nd R) your own notes,

- **R**ecite (3rd R) what you have written,

- **R**evise (4th R) the material frequently.

▶ **Take Responsibility:** Understand that YOU and only YOU are answerable and responsible for your deeds. Stop blaming your parents.

▶ **Define your own principles** and stand by them. Never allow your friends to manipulate or dictate terms. Though they might laugh at you, you must assertively say, "No" to your friends if required.

▶ **Bite the hard nut first:** When you feel the first rush of energy, do the strenuous and challenging tasks that appear first on the to-do list.

▶ **Sleep well:** 7-8 hours of sleep is appropriate for a student. Below 5 hours of rest has proved to slow down the brain.

▶ **Return of Investment:** Make sure you read the syllabus book before the text book! Identify the top marks fetchers and concentrate on them first. This is only during exam time.

▶ **Ask:** We Indians like giving advice. The problem is nobody is ready to take it! Go reach out to people and ask for solutions to your problems. Don't wait until you are doing badly in a class and have to catch up.

"Even if you're on the right track, you'll get run over if you just sit there." – *Will Rogers*

▶ **Reward Yourself:** Whenever you accomplish a chunk of tasks, reward yourself with a piece of candy or a small reward.

▶ **Don't sell books:** There is a common practice of selling off the previous academic year's books. Stop it. They might be useful for future reference.

▶ **Pray and meditate: A** study says that praying/meditating for a mere 10 minutes a day boosts your morale and helps in de-stressing your body. Make it a routine activity.

▶ **Not a supercomputer:** If at all you need a PC or a laptop, let it be an instrument which can just run vital software. You do not need the fastest, greatest or latest comp in town.

▶ **Math can't be read:** *Suhas used to fluently read the problems in the Math text book.* Math problems need to be solved on a daily basis to master the subject. Reading to comprehend Math is like watching YouTube videos to learn swimming.

▶ **Speed up:** If there is too much information to study in little time, skip these three obstacles of speed reading:

1. Finger Tracing On the Page: Trace the material with your eyes, not with your finger. If you slide your finger through the page to keep track of where you are studying, you are wasting time. The speed of eyes and finger are similar to the speed of lightning and thunder, in the same order.

2. Vocalising: Since childhood we have been forced to vocalise while studying, so that our elders can

check if we are studying or dozing off! Now that you have grown up, stop that habit which consumes time and energy.

3. <u>Body rocking</u>: You are not a doll in a gift store to keep rocking back and forth. Instead of shaking your leg, neck and other parts of the body, study in a comfortable static posture to save time and energy. Your mind's efficiency lowers with increased multitasking.

Exam Hints:

Handling multiple choice questions:

- Don't guess in a flash! The challenge is to find the best answer, not the correct answer.

- A study says that 65% of 'all of the above' or 'none of the above' options tend to be correct.

- Beware the terms such as: 'never', 'always', 'ensures', 'may sometimes be', 'will never be', 'guarantees', etc. Their presence can change the meaning of a statement.

- Heed grammatical clues such as 'an', 'are', etc. to guess the number of options.

- If you are in a dilemma about an answer, try reverse engineering, in which you eliminate the improbable options.

- If there is no negative marking and you are clueless about a question, choose the options **B** or **C**. A study shows that your chance of getting it right is quite high! *But don't try this for all the questions!*

The night before the exam:

- Revise all the *Naughty-Notes* you had prepared earlier along with the textbook.

- Get your bag ready with the required stationeries, hall-ticket, calculator, water bottle, etc.

- Have a light dinner and go to bed early. Sleep for at least 7-8 hours.

The day of the exam:

- Set your alarm and get up early. Allow ample time to reach the hall 15 minutes prior to the exam.

- Don't skip breakfast. Eat a light yet energizing breakfast including a fruit, and light carbohydrates like a *chapatti*. In addition, as caffeine has been proven to increase alertness, drink a cup if you have the habit.

- **Don't study new topics.** Simply glance through your notes and textbook.

- If you are tense, relax, take deep breaths, and be confident about your preparation and chill. Be cautious about 'anxiety friends' who pressurize you about improbable topics and questions!

During the exam:

- Carefully understand all the instructions on the booklet.

- Have a bird's eye view of the questions you will attempt. Start with the answers you know best.

- Keep an eye on the clock. Avoid focussing on one question and therefore running out of time on the others.

- Never lend or borrow anything from your neighbor without permission of the invigilator. Clear the memory of the calculator before lending.

- Check for any paper bits or any documents in your pouch or pocket. Your carelessness may turn out to be an expensive mistake.

- Don't attract the attention of the invigilator by yawing loudly, staring, bending down for a long time, pretending to sleep, hoodwinking or playing smart games, chewing, holding the answer sheet on your lap, etc. Realise that he/she is a facilitator for the exam and don't taunt him/her to turn into an invigilator.

- Listen to all the instructions and warning bell rings.

- If a squad member interrogates you during a random check, remain calm and answer calmly. Don't panic, regret or growl.

- Ensure that you have entered your name and/or register number on the exam sheet. There is no use in scoring a distinction without your name on it.

- Utilise the whole exam period rather than rushing through the test. Try completing 15 minutes before the final bell to revise.

Don't study to become an engineer in an MNC or a doctor in a multi-specialty hospital. Study to learn. Study to scale up and improve the system. Study to improve the country.

The pleasure of being a Narayan Murthy or a Kiran Bedi is immeasurable.

What happened next?

By the time the final exams of 9th standard got finished, I was also finished!

April 10th was the results. We had to collect the marks card WITH our parents.

As usual I was accompanied by mom, and she was mentally prepared to take the criticism. I warned her not to create a scene in the staff room like the last time.

Mrs. Sunitha welcomed us with an unusual smile. This was the second time in my life I had seen her smile – her first smile in class was by mistake.

"*Thees ees* the boy I *waas taaking* about. A failure student in the midterm *exaam* has scored a *respacttable* 81% in the final *exaam*!" she said to the school principal in a fluent flow.

I thought she was making fun of me. But when I saw my mom proudly receiving the marks card from Mrs. Sunitha, I had to pinch myself. Mom smeared the boldly written '81%' on the marks card, and squeezed my chin firmly with the same hand. She was happy. I didn't want anything else then; I had got what I wanted.

"Chandan, *haw cood* you *acheeve thees*?" Mrs. Sunitha asked and smiled for the third time.

"That's a secret, Ma'am!" I said.

Life is certainly a full circle.